THE IFBB ALBUM OF
BODYBUILDING
ALL-STARS

THE IFBB ALBUM OF BODYBUILDING ALL-STARS

JOE WEIDER

Introduction by **BEN WEIDER, C.M.**
Foreword by **MIKE MENTZER, Mr. Universe**

HAWTHORN BOOKS, INC.
Publishers/New York
A Howard & Wyndham Company

This book was conceived and edited by Bob Oskam

Designed by Millicent Fairhurst

CONTENTS

FOREWORD

All the beauty and sublimity we have bestowed upon real and imaginary things I
will reclaim as the product and property of man as his fairest apology.

–Friederich Nietzsche

"Why did you ever take up bodybuilding in the first place?" This is the
question most often asked me by the media since I won the Mr.
America contest in October of 1976. Being pressed for an immediate
reply in the typical interview, I first found myself repeating the apt
retort of Sir Edmund Hillary, Mt. Everest's conqueror, "Because it was
there." This, of course, implies that the mere challenge of molding the
human form is explanation enough, but more serious reflection sug-
gests much deeper and more complicated motives.

My abiding love and passion for bodybuilding began with a muscle
magazine at a hometown newsstand when I was just twelve years old.
When my eyes caught that cover shot of Bill Pearl, the man who may
have inspired more young men to take up bodybuilding than any
other competitor, I knew I too would become a "muscle man." My
contemporaries looked to ball players and movie celebrities as role
models, but I, a young, starry-eyed romantic, saw physique champions as the masculine ideal.

Of course, as my physique and psyche have matured, my motives
for continuing bodybuilding have evolved as well. No longer fettered
by adolescent identity conflicts, my energies are liberated and seek
their expression in competence and maturation as a top-level competitive athlete. The sweat, toil, and self-discipline required in this
pursuit of excellence mold the character; winning or losing is second-
ary in importance. The goal is no longer to be like someone else.
Rather, it is to be more fully myself—to achieve the potential I feel
within me.

The difficult process of attaining peak physical and mental condition in preparation for competition determines whether the individual
competitor will succeed and move further into the foreground, or fail
and recede into anonymity.

Probably the best example of bodybuilding success is Arnold
Schwarzenegger. It would be a gross error of omission to discuss
bodybuilding without referring to him. When Joe Weider brought the
Wunderkind to southern California from Austria to train and promote him, Arnold could scarcely utter a word of English. Today,
some ten years later, he is a millionaire, building a successful career as
an actor in English-speaking movies. Besides all this, he won the Mr.
Olympia contest six times in succession, 1970 through 1975, without

ever seriously being challenged. Arnold is the first to admit that the discipline he cultivated to help him succeed so spectacularly in bodybuilding is largely responsible for his subsequent achievements in business and acting.

Arnold's stellar ascent to the zenith of the bodybuilding world has provided the necessary excitement to draw an increasingly interested public. That public, still reeling from a decade of intense social change that has seen the easing of rigid role distinctions between men and women, the resurrection of the physical hero, and a renewed interest in health, fitness, and physical appearance, has come to see Arnold as the embodiment of a newly found value system. Now we see ourselves in an age of the self—self-reliance, self-confidence, self-actualization.

With Arnold at the center of bodybuilding's heightened public profile, the current generation of bodybuilders finds an unprecedented opportunity for career advancement and personal achievements, beyond what even Arnold accomplished. Bodybuilding is on the verge of an exciting leap into professionalism. When Arnold won his final Mr. Olympia title in 1975 at Pretoria, South Africa, he received a meager $1,000. When he began promoting the Mr. Olympia in 1976, the prize money was increased to $3,500. It has grown each year, until this year, 1979, the first-place award is $20,000, with $30,000 more to be divided among the other place winners. This is just the beginning. Ben Weider, IFBB president, has organized a professional tour with eight additional contests to be held in 1979. Total cash prizes will range between $150,000 and $200,000. Ben's prospectus for 1980 calls for at least twelve professional contests to be held all over the world in Grand Prix fashion, with top money winners competing at year's end for some fabulous, as yet unannounced, Grand Prix bonus. Total cash prizes for 1980 could reach as high as $500,000!

Sources of income already established for professionals include exhibition appearances, seminars, personal endorsements, and mail-order sales of training materials, as well as the occasional windfall movie part or television commercial. In the next two years top professionals will pull in $250,000 to $500,000 annually. Of course all of this is self-generating too, just as tennis only became popular when its professionals started to become top money makers. One day the picture of a professional bodybuilder might even appear on the cover of *Sports Illustrated*. Then who will dare ask the bodybuilder why he ever took up the sport in the first place?

But making money is not necessarily bodybuilding's *summum bonum*. In the last year and a half I have been to Europe six times, and to Hawaii, Mexico, and Canada, as well as all over the good ole U.S.A. Other "perks" include the interesting people you unavoidably meet, lots of publicity, and, while I haven't used my physique to attract sexual partners, there are those who find that a healthy, muscular body makes such contacts more available. And we must not forget the ego gratification that is part and parcel of possessing a set of muscles.

I feel certain that when all is said and done and I measure my "bodybuilding period" against a lifetime of experience, it will stand out as much more than just a transitory interlude. Look at the later years of some of my heroic forebears, most of whom appear in this book. In addition to making transitions to other full-time vocations and careers as actors, businessmen, lawyers, and entrepreneurs, many have remained devoted to the wonderful sport-art of bodybuilding; they have a spiritual affinity to the sport, not just a physical one. I am proud to be carrying on the great tradition of excellence they have so clearly established.

—Mike Mentzer
Mr. Universe, Mr. America

PREFACE

The photographs that appear in this book are but a small fraction of the total that I've accumulated in my years as publisher of *Muscle Builder* magazine and as trainer of bodybuilding champions. In making the selection here, I have tried consciously to give a sense of the development of bodybuilding in this century. Consequently, this book does to some extent serve as a visual history of the sport. In these pages you will see tremendous changes in the men over the years, made possible through the application of scientific training and nutritional principles that I and others have discovered in the course of the past decades. Today's champions are able to achieve bulk and muscularity, with sharp definition, that was beyond the reach of those training in years past. But it took a Sandow, a Goodrich, a Thériault to provide the foundations on which we've built, so it is fitting and proper that these men and their contemporaries be accorded recognition here.

Also in the photo selection that follows, you will note that I present a diversified view of the bodybuilder and his world. I have done this for two specific reasons: first, so that the cumulative impression is not a static one; second, to provide a sense not only of the beauty of each male figure, but also of the necessary effort exerted in achieving the potential inherent in the body, and of the joy that accompanies the achievement. For this has an effect on the whole experience of life; it is not limited to the confines of this one sport.

This is a look at bodybuilding through the experience of those who have truly excelled in it. You will see the acknowledgment of that excellence through the eyes of photographers who have captured classic moments of artistic beauty, spontaneous as well as posed. You will see it in the moments of victory and triumph recorded here, although this is by no means a complete record of each man's competitive achievements—this volume is not intended as such. Each man merits his own story, but here each plays but a part in the one story of modern bodybuilding.

There is a close camaraderie within the bodybuilding world. Despite an intense striving on the part of each man to surpass his fellow, there remains an underlying fraternity and mutual respect. The sport encourages this. And because I feel these traits must be encouraged and developed throughout society if we are to be and remain strong as people and nations, I particularly hope you will note the evidence of them presented here.

It has been my great privilege to meet and know most of the men featured in this book. Their determination, and that of all who train as bodybuilders, to explore fully the potential and the limits of the body, has earned for bodybuilding its position of respect in the world of athletics. I wish to record here my esteem and my appreciation for the dedication these men have shown in their endeavor and for the cooperation they have shown me in my efforts to promote bodybuilding as an athletic science and a recognized competitive sport.

I wish also to express my personal gratitude to the staff of *Muscle Builder* magazine for their unstinting support and cooperation. In particular I want to thank feature editor Armand Tanny, editor-in-chief Bill Reynolds, and European and world champion Mike Mentzer, who have done much of the research behind this book; and I thank as well staff photographers Jimmy Caruso, Artie Zeller, Craig Dietz, and John Balik, whose sense of artistry and creativity are so evident in the pages of photographs that follow. A note of thanks as well to Wayne DeMilia for his assistance in the preparation of the photo captions.

THE IFBB ALBUM OF BODYBUILDING ALL-STARS

INTRODUCTION: FIRST, THE CULTURE OF THE BODY

A Capsule History of the International Federation of Bodybuilders

by Ben Weider, C.M., International President

"First, the culture of the body," wrote Baron Pierre de Coubertin in the process of setting down the foundations for the modern Olympic Games. His sentiments live on, but what a pity that the baron himself did not survive long enough to witness the advent of the International Federation of Bodybuilders, the fiercely dedicated group that, within a relatively short period, has established itself as one of the leading sports organizations in the world.

Not so long ago, shortly after I returned home from a tour of the Soviet Union that in itself was further proof of the influence of our sport throughout the world, I was guest of honor at a major bodybuilding promotion in Columbus, Ohio. Some five thousand excited fans had traveled from all over the United States and Canada to witness the event. Indeed, tickets to the promotion had disappeared a full five months earlier, and now scalpers were enjoying a brisk trade outside the theater.

Also conspicuously present were reporters from *New West* magazine, *Rolling Stone*, *Newsweek*, and *New Age*, not to mention various daily newspapers from around the country. One woman I spoke with assured me that she had been sent all the way from Germany to cover the proceedings for *Stern*. And one could not miss the team from ABC television, with cameras strategically positioned so as not to miss the least bit of this exciting program.

As the master of ceremonies approached his microphone, a loud roar rose from the crowd in the packed auditorium in eager anticipation of the night to remember that the published program had promised. Audience enthusiasm for bodybuilding these days knows no limits. This particular crowd had looked forward to the show for a whole year, and now it was letting its idols know in no uncertain terms how it felt about their achievements. In truth, this was no different from the way opera fans, Mick Jagger supporters, or followers of Reggie Jackson might behave at a performance by their particular hero.

The master of ceremonies, resplendent in blue tuxedo, came to the microphone. He raised his hand for peace, and as the audience quieted down, said, "Ladies and gentlemen, it gives me great pleasure to welcome you to our show tonight, but before I announce the first of our stars, let me retrace our steps a little, back to the early days of the International Federation."

I could hardly believe the reaction to this simple announcement, for far from displaying impatience with the master of ceremonies, fans exploded with enthusiasm for what had been offered. It seems that the story of the IFBB, this group that has over the years become synonymous with *organized* bodybuilding, is as exciting to the followers of our sport as are the contests themselves.

Yes, Baron Pierre de Coubertin would have been proud of our achievements. In fact, there is no doubt in my mind that were he alive today, bodybuilding would now be an important part of the Olympic program. The spark that he struck has ignited an interest in the culture of the body that not even the baron could have foreseen during the many years he was president of the International Olympic Committee.

With the introduction of the modern Olympics, the interest in physical development that had waned with the decline of the Roman and Greek civilizations, blossomed once again. People began to show renewed enthusiasm for strength performances, and by the 1920s small groups were staging bodybuilding contests in France, Belgium, England, and the United States. The greater number of these events were presented in music halls and nightclubs, and consequently regarded as little more than freak shows by the drunken patrons. At best, the shows were regarded as male beauty contests, something that was fun to watch, something to laugh at—like circus clowns. Not surprisingly, few people at that time considered bodybuilding a sport.

But then came 1947 and the winds that heralded a change in attitudes toward bodybuilding. With much help from my brother Joe, I organized the first Mr. Canada physique contest. Steve Reeves, who was possibly the leading bodybuilder of the time and on his way to becoming a very successful movie star, was our special guest. We had rented the Monument National Theatre in downtown Montreal with monies received from the advance sale of tickets, but my brother and I had not anticipated the success of our first promotion. In fact, we filled every one of the theater's thirteen hundred seats and were forced to turn away over a thousand disappointed fans.

If we needed proof of bodybuilding's potential, here it was before our very eyes. Shortly after the Mr. Canada contest, Joe and I decided to join the Amateur Athletic Union (AAU), which was in control of bodybuilding in Canada at the time. We were convinced that if we got together with the AAU to help promote bodybuilding in the right

Ben Weider, C.M., President of the International Federation of Bodybuilders, receiving the Order of Canada from the Governor General of Canada, the Honourable Jules Leger. The Order of Canada is the highest award the Canadian government can bestow upon its citizens for contributions to humanity through specific activities. Mr. Weider was honored for his thirty-two years of work in building the IFBB into the seventh largest amateur sports federation in the world, and his commendation reflects the position of respect achieved by bodybuilding as an internationally recognized competitive sport.

way, the sport could reach levels of public acceptance hardly anticipated by those then in control. Unfortunately, we came up against too much selfishness and short-sightedness, and Joe and I decided instead to form a group that was interested solely in the promotion of bodybuilding. "First, the culture of the body" indeed.

We called our little group the International Federation of Bodybuilders (IFBB), with just two member nations, Canada and the United States.

Our federation received a great boost from the popular American champions of the time. Many of them had been neglected by promoters, who seemed more interested in promoting weightlifting and used bodybuilding only to attract the hordes to their first love. Clarence Ross, Alan Stephan, and Ed Thériault are just some of the big bodybuilders of the late 1940s who put their confidence in the dream that Joe and I sought to achieve. Without the efforts of men like these, at a time when the sport of bodybuilding was largely neglected by the press and existing sports organizations we certainly would not have established ourselves as quickly as we did.

It was also in 1947 that I started traveling around the world to encourage bodybuilders to form national federations and organize national contests. Such was my success in this venture that by 1964, forty-three nations had chosen to affiliate with the IFBB.

In those days the International Weightlifting Federation also staged bodybuilding events. This caused much confusion and tended to impede progress. But with the relinquishment of all bodybuilding interests in 1969, the IWF left the way clear for IFBB's growth. Now those nations who were affiliated with the IWF turned en masse to the IFBB: Bodybuilding continued to grow.

In 1970 the IFBB joined the General Assembly of International Sports Federations, based in Monaco, which was formed for the coordination of Olympic and non-Olympic amateur sport. All international federations joined GAISF. With the acquisition of membership in that group, IFBB support rose to unprecedented levels—by 1974 seventy-two nations had become affiliated.

At the 1978 IFBB Congress, held in Acapulco, Mexico, under the sponsorship of the Honorable Guillermo Lopez Portillo, Director of the Mexico Sports Confederation (INDE), the IFBB added Libya and Colombia, increasing its ranks to a whopping 103 members. The IFBB is consequently the seventh strongest international amateur sports federation in the world.

The IFBB has attracted to its executive staff many talented people who are dedicated to the principles laid down by Baron de Coubertin so many years ago. Oscar State of London, for years associated with the Olympic Games, is a famous sports administrator who now helps guide the IFBB to greater levels of achievement. Dennis Stallard, a well-respected sports official in the United Kingdom, is helping the IFBB improve its judging procedures. As a direct consequence of the untiring work of the IFBB executive staff and its various vice-presidents around the world, bodybuilding will be an important part of the Asian Games.

The acceptance of bodybuilding as a worthwhile sport is evident. Visnews, the largest television news agency in the world, annually sends a five-minute review of bodybuilding news to more than ninety-eight countries. Such exposure has done our sport untold good. In the United States, ABC's "Wide World of Sports" has for many years given IFBB promotions wonderful coverage. CBS covered the 1978

IFBB World Championships in Mexico. The CBS film was viewed by millions throughout North America and the rest of the world.

Lately the IFBB has turned its hand toward making the sport more lucrative for professional bodybuilders. First, Joe Weider created the Mr. Olympia contest, which would soon become known throughout the world as bodybuilding's Super Bowl. At first the Mr. Olympia prize money totalled just $1,000. Today, contenders share a staggering $50,000 and look forward to even larger purses in the near future. Already, more professional contests are being planned that will make well in excess of $200,000 available to the professionals in a year or so.

With up to forty-three member nations represented in the annual IFBB World Championships, the group has decided to stage the event in a different country each year. I have always prided myself on keeping politics out of sport, since it is my firm belief that the United Nations can adequately deal with the world's political problems. Sports and politics do not make good bedfellows, and politicians should not be allowed the opportunity to use a sport to further their political careers. Every year, the IFBB Congress accommodates representatives of every religious denomination and every political persuasion. Ours is truly a brotherhood dedicated to the well-being of man.

Chairman Mao Tse-Tung once wrote, "Develop physical culture and sport to build up the health of the people." Our sentiments exactly.

General Carlos Romulo, former foreign secretary of the Philippines, once told me, "Bodybuilding is important for nation-building." His words are now the motto of the IFBB.

It remains now to give thanks to those early champions who placed their faith and the future of their sport in my brother's hands and in mine. Without their cooperation in those crucial early days, bodybuilding might not have progressed as rapidly as it has.

Special thanks must go to Joe Weider and his *Muscle Builder* magazine staff, in particular to Rick Wayne, a champion in his own right whose idiosyncratic style of reporting has captured the popular imagination. Rick Wayne's contribution to our sport cannot possibly be measured.

Then there are today's heroes: Arnold Schwarzenegger, Franco Columbu, Mike Mentzer, and too many others to mention here, who in their own way have done so much for the furtherance of this sport of ours, and who by their examples have turned a whole world on to the concept of *first, the culture of the body.*

We certainly have come a long way.

EUGENE SANDOW

Frederick Mueller, the man who later became known as Eugene Sandow, was born in Konigsburg, East Prussia, on April 2, 1867. Mingled fact and fancy about this early muscle star still plague his fans. During his life, press agentry described him as a weak and sickly lad, but no early information indicates that he was anything but normally healthy. We now know that his father, an alleged gem merchant (so the hype went), was actually a fruit-and-vegetable huckster.

Sandow had none of the girth and mass of the modern muscleman, but he was a living inspiration to people of his day, who believed he was the strongest and best built man in the world. His has been the seminal influence leading up to modern bodybuilding, the cult of massive muscle and sculptured physique. More than one hundred ten years after his birth, his achievements are still remembered.

While in England in 1889, Sandow won a contest of strength against Charles Sampson, self-styled "strongest man in the world," and for the next four years he parlayed that title to stellar engagements in the better halls and theaters of England, Australia, South Africa, and Continental Europe. During this time his brand of physical culture spread to police and fire departments and to schools.

A then unknown promoter named Flo Ziegfeld saw Sandow's act at the Casino Theatre on New York's Broadway in 1893 and signed him for ten weeks at the Chicago World's Fair. Chicago went wild over Sandow, and Ziegfeld (not yet famous for his follies) signed the glamorous German strongman to a four-year management contract.

Sandow was a natty dresser and assumed a manner of highbrow charm. At San Francisco's Stockwell Theater he posed for the "ladies only" audiences decked in a silk G-string. The *Chronicle* on May 17, 1894, wrote: "The ladies lingered about the door in order to see in street attire this modern Hercules, to whom a collar is a profanation."

In two years of touring, Sandow made a quarter of a million dollars for Ziegfeld.

Returning to England, Sandow set up four gyms and opened a lucrative mail-order business selling training equipment. Exercise, said Sandow, was one of the best forms of treatment for many diseases. He was way ahead of his time.

He promoted a Perfect Man Contest, open to the men of the United Kingdom. It took him two years to round up the best. In the finals at Albert Hall in London, winner W. L. Murray was awarded a gold statuette of Sandow and a big cash prize. Thus was born the physique show as we know it today.

Sandow was a masterful showman with ultimate posing control. Given today's training systems, I feel he would likely have won the Mr. Olympia title.

GEORGE HACKENSCHMIDT

George Hackenschmidt was born in Dorpat, Estonia—now part of the USSR—on July 20, 1877. By the time he was fourteen years old he was into weight training, and as a schoolboy he won many gymnastic meets. He weighed all of 122 pounds.

He broke world weightlifting records and also became the world's leading wrestler at the beginning of this century. His physique had great box-office appeal, and he kept in top condition far into his old age.

Hack learned weight training from Czar Nicholas's personal physician, Dr. von Krajewski, and served five months with the First Life Guards of His Majesty. By the time he was twenty, Hack was able to military press 279¾ pounds, one-hand-bent press 286 pounds, and power clean 361 pounds.

He began to compete all over Europe, lifting and wrestling. He always won, and his popularity put him in the same income bracket as Eugene Sandow, earning him as much as $1,750 a week (equal to $15,000 now). He was known as the Russian Lion, though when stranded in France in 1939 by World War II, he became a naturalized French citizen. At age seventy-four, after forty years of trying, he became a British subject.

Hack defended his World Wrestling Championship against the Terrible Turk in London in 1904 in a bout that captured public imagination. It was over in seconds: Hack slammed the Turk to the ground, dislocating his opponent's shoulder. He went on to beat the American Tom Jenkins twice, but with the mighty Frank Gotch the going was tougher, and Hack badly injured his knee, never to wrestle again.

After that he wrote several scholarly books—*The Science of Living, Man and Yourself, Consciousness and Character*, and others. He was in demand as a lecturer in universities all over Europe, and he could speak French, German, and Russian fluently, as well as English. He took part in public debates with George Bernard Shaw.

Inventive, he devised the Hack lift machine, still a popular piece of gym equipment. He had phenomenal leg power, and in his eighties could still jump over the back of a chair fifty times in fast succession and do miles of roadwork each week.

When Hack was in his prime, his physique was photographed, painted, and sculpted by famous artists, and his name was a household word. In 1952, Hack still thrilled Muscle Beach, California, with his visit.

He died in London on February 19, 1968. He had given away most of his trophies—his gold medals had gone to a dentist friend who found difficulty getting gold for fillings during the war years.

Photo taken in Johannesburg in 1907.

A rare photo of Hackenschmidt at twenty-one years of age.

9

SIEGMUND KLEIN

Siegmund Klein was born in what was then Germany (Thorn, West Prussia) on April 19, 1902. His family emigrated to Cleveland, Ohio, in 1903. He learned to love strength activities from his powerful father, and he became a well-known athlete in Cleveland. He moved to New York City in 1924 and opened a gym at 207 West 48th Street, later moving it to 717 Seventh Avenue. The atmosphere was heavy with muscle lore—pictures of famous physical culturists, ancient stage barbells mixed with more modern equipment, and an extensive collection of beer steins lining the walls. The gym combined the muscle culture of earlier Europe with that of more modern America.

Klein subscribed more to bodybuilding and posing than to strength, and he coined the famous phrase that remains valid to this day: "Train for shape, and strength will follow."

A dedicated collector, he turned the dining room of his New York town house into a replica of an old German tavern, complete with furniture and pictures. It included part of his collection of beer steins, each of which depicted strongmen, lifters, and muscular marvels.

In 1925 Klein won the French Beaute Plastique contest for the world's best-built athlete. Sig's fine abdominal development, which he said he built using his own invention, the "in-Klein board," was particularly remarked on.

He was featured eight times in Ripley's famous "Believe-It-Or-Not" columns. In 1945 his measurements were the following: height, 5 feet 4 inches; weight, 150 pounds; chest, 44 inches; waist, 31; thigh, 22; and biceps, 15¾. He was still a popular performer. In 1947 he gave a nostalgic and historic posing exhibition in Los Angeles. He was a master of fluid muscle control, in contrast to the rock-hard, static posing today.

Klein promoted bodybuilding for half a century in the heart of New York City's theater district. He inspired and trained thousands of people in his small gym over the years. The Sandow influence was strong: Huge photographs of the famous showman looked down from every part of the studio. In 1973 Sig Klein closed the gym and liquidated his vast muscle virtu to private collectors.

BERT GOODRICH

Bert Goodrich was the first official Mr. America, winning the title at Amsterdam, New York, in 1939. He was born in Phoenix, Arizona, in 1907. As a boy he romped in the rugged southwest terrain—rode horses, swam in rivers and ponds, and played all the games rural kids were known to play. By the time he entered high school he was a dazzling athlete. His structure, speed, and instinctive athletic ability were reminiscent of the great Jim Thorpe.

A veritable physical dynamo with a lifelong insatiable appetite for sports, Goodrich could sprint, dive, ski, swim, box, ice-skate, hand-balance, tumble, and lift weights with the best of them. In fact, at thirty-eight years of age he ran the hundred-yard dash in 9.8 seconds. And as the Athletic Chief Petty Officer at the San Diego Naval Base during World War II, he was never bested in the sprint by any recruit who trained under him.

Goodrich became interested in building more muscle in his late teens and started with the Earle Liederman cable training course. After high school he went to Arizona State College, and during the summer breaks trained with professional handbalancing and tumbling acts. He even took up boxing and fought many professional bouts at 185 pounds bodyweight.

He turned to professional handbalancing after college and worked the cabaret circuit nationwide. He also developed a single handbalancing act and barnstormed with circuses and fairs. He did a frightening trick—a handbalance atop a 125-foot pole on a pair of bicycle handlebars.

The excitement and profit of movie stunt work drew Bert to Hollywood, and he doubled for the likes of Johnny Weismuller, Buster Crabbe, Victor McLaglen, George Brent, and many others. He fell off cliffs, raced motorcycles, and leaped chasms. Broken bones were no deterrent. He also did a handbalancing act on ice.

Goodrich married Norma Tanny, sister of well-known Vic and Armand Tanny, and he co-promoted the legendary first professional Mr. USA show with Vic Tanny. In Hollywood in 1947 he opened a beautiful gym which became a health mecca for movie stars. He opened five more gyms but later sold out.

Still athletic at seventy-one, weighing well over 200 pounds, he kicks into a one-hand stand at will. He also lifts weights, rides a bike, and does wind sprints. He has competed in the Senior Olympic exhibitions. He is often featured on television talk shows.

He lives in Canoga Park, California, in semiretirement.

13

At 220 pounds bodyweight.

Sharing a light moment with actor friend Cesar Romero.

Performing the difficult "flag" stunt with George Redpath, mid-1930s.

JOHN GRIMEK

In the Depression era, when giants such as Franklin D. Roosevelt and King Kong provided America with heroes of great intellectual or physical stature, John Grimek provided an incarnate compromise—a flesh-and-blood hero whom muscle celebrants took to their hearts. Of Czechoslovakian stock, he was a man out of middle America who, with his great muscular mass, fine structure, masterful posing, and engaging personality, heralded the modern era of bodybuilding.

He was born in Perth Amboy, New Jersey, in 1909, and began weightlifting at a young age. When he was twenty, grainy, sensational pictures of him dominated the flimsy editions of early physical culture publications. His fame grew through the 1930s with his continued exposure in *Strength & Health* magazine, of which he eventually became editor. During that period, he trained mostly for competition weightlifting and in 1936 became the American heavyweight champion representing the United States at the Berlin Olympic Games. He traveled the country, giving weightlifting and posing exhibitions. Powerful, agile, and flexible, he gave handbalancing and contortion exhibitions that included feats of strength and posing through which he dispelled forever the illusion that men of muscle were not athletes.

In 1940, the Grimek name rocketed and went into permanent orbit with his AAU Mr. America victory. He was thirty-one years old. He repeated the victory in 1941, and when it became clear that he might never be defeated, it was ruled that thereafter a man could win the title only once.

In 1948, at the age of thirty-nine, he overwhelmed the London audience with his Mr. Universe victory over the young, phenomenal Mr. America, Steve Reeves. Grimek weighed 203 pounds with chest, 50 inches; waist, 30½; biceps, 18½.

The following year in Los Angeles he won the 1949 Mr. USA title at the Shrine Auditorium before a packed house of seven thousand, facing the most formidable physiques of the time: Clarence Ross, Steve Reeves, George Eiferman, and Armand Tanny. With this professional victory Grimek retired, the only bodybuilder in history who was never defeated in a contest.

With full control of every muscle, flexible to the extreme, Grimek exuded power in his posing. Few bodybuilders have approached his charisma or the perfection of his routine. Powerful, too, he could jerk 370 pounds overhead and simultaneously press two dumbbells weighing 110 and 125 pounds.

A happy, dedicated family man, he lives in York, Pennsylvania, where he continues to write about bodybuilding training. Still massive, still strong at age seventy, celebrated and revered, he remains living proof of the benefits of lifelong training.

Although he has had no formal association with the IFBB, we who are with the IFBB regard him as a great world champion whose record and photographs are properly a part of an album of bodybuilding all-stars.

Mr. USA 1949.

Mr. America 1940.

20

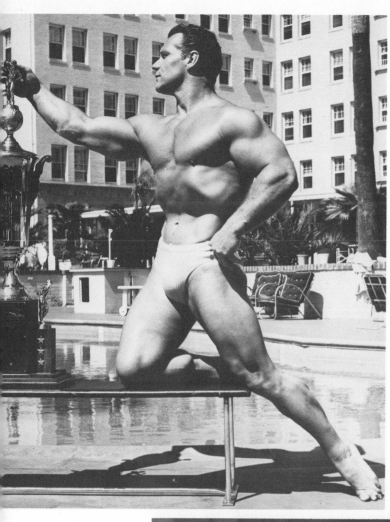

Guest posing at Carnegie Hall.

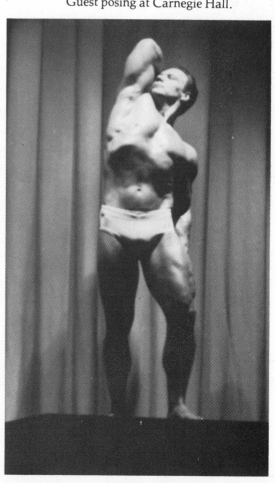

CLARENCE ROSS

Clarence (Clancy) Ross zoomed to fame when he won the Mr. America title in 1945 at the close of World War II. During the war years millions of young men had been exposed to physical conditioning, and many to formal bodybuilding. Ross, still in the air force, was the epitome of muscular development through training. Lean, defined, and handsome, he became a hero in the fast-expanding bodybuilding community. After leaving the service later that year, he set up his own gym in Alameda, California, and bodybuilders throughout the nation beat a path to his door.

Clancy dominated the muscle magazines of the era with innumerable cover pictures, training articles, and photos illustrating many bodybuilding courses and products. He was truly in the vanguard of the modern bodybuilding movement. He traveled extensively, giving exhibitions, and his posing routines were unforgettable. He could hit successive poses rapidly for ten minutes without repeating any of them.

In 1948 Ross accomplished what people today find hard to believe: He beat the magnificent Steve Reeves for the Mr. USA title before a turn-away crowd of seven thousand at the Shrine Auditorium in Los Angeles. To this day no greater bodybuilding audience has been recorded. Ross also won the $1,000 prize, the first sizable amount ever paid to a professional title winner.

The following year Ross again placed above Reeves in the Mr. USA contest, held at the Shrine before another capacity crowd, but Ross had to be content with second place behind the popular, venerable winner, John Grimek.

Ross's career was spotty from that time on. Although he had twice beaten Reeves, he was beaten also—in 1955 by the superb Canadian Léo Robert at the Mr. Universe contest, and again in the 1956 Mr. USA contest by the upcoming all-time great, Bill Pearl.

Ross relinquished his gym to become a manager with the short-lived American Health Studios chain. He became a district newspaper manager after that, a job he held for many years. More recently he opened another highly successful gym of his own and is reported to be in excellent physical shape.

During his peak years, Clancy's measurements were chest, 49½ inches; arms, 17¾; thighs, 26; calves, 16½; waist, 31½.

Demonstrating a new line of weight-training equipment with Steve Reeves.

ALAN STEPHAN

The dark horse winner of the 1946 Mr. America title was handsome, blond Alan Stephan. Although he was comparatively unknown when he competed in navy weightlifting competition (1943–46), his striking looks won him transferral to publicity and recruiting work. He was the powerful man in the navy poster displayed everywhere in America exhorting young men to "Man the Guns." The poster showed Stephan stripped to the waist, holding a live 85-pound shell, and offered a preview of later physique photographs of this muscular Adonis.

Born and raised in politically turbulent Cicero, Illinois, and insulated by his doting family from the tight, tense environment there, Alan grew into a happy, gangling youngster. The genetics of his physique were evident only in his immigrant father, who boasted a 22½-inch arm resulting from farm toil in his native Lithuania and steel mill work in Indiana.

He started weight training in high school, and after graduation in 1943 he joined the navy. He volunteered for the Seabees and was assigned as a judo, wrestling, and physical training instructor. He finished his enlistment in Guam two months before winning the Mr. America title. In beating the popular stars of the day, Sam Loprinzi, Joe Lauriana, Kimon Voyages, Gene Jantzen, and Vic Nicoletti, he received 74 out of a possible 75 points.

Stephan's bodybuilding fame obscured his weightlifting ability. He did a straight arm pullover with 200 pounds, curled 205 pounds eight reps, and did a 420 squat for six reps.

At the age of twenty-two he stood 5 feet 11½ inches at a weight of 205 pounds, with chest 50¼ inches; waist 31½; biceps, 18⅛; thighs, 26; calves, 17.

His striking handsomeness and flashing smile led him to Hollywood, where he went to study acting. The movie career he had hoped for did not materialize, but he did receive a lot of worthwhile publicity. He opened a health studio in Minneapolis, Minnesota, and did well. He later joined a gym syndicate and little has been heard of him since.

The original oil painting for the navy poster was hung in the Navy Department in Washington, the only likeness of an enlisted man amidst a sea of admirals' portraits.

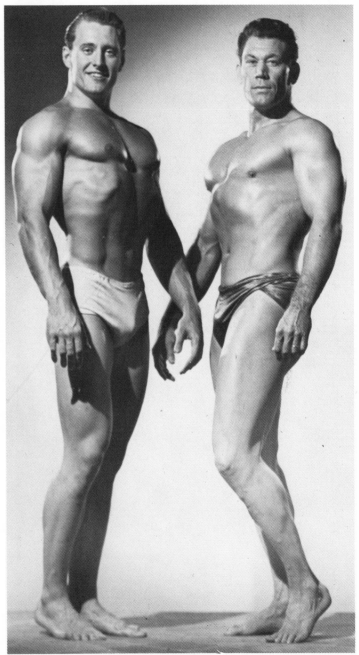

Stephan posing with Bert Goodrich.

IFBB Mr. America 1949 being congratulated by IFBB President Ben Weider. Stephan also received the Most Muscular Man trophy in this contest.

STEVE REEVES

The incomparable Steve Reeves began bodybuilding at age sixteen in Ed Yarick's Gym in Oakland, California. Born in Glasgow, Montana, on January 21, 1927, he spent much time during his early years on horseback, an interest he still pursues. Six feet tall, broad-shouldered (23½ inches across), 212 pounds, perfectly proportioned and stunningly handsome, he made an enormous impact on the muscle culture in 1947 with his first major victory, the Mr. America title. Even as a soldier in the Philippines, where he saw action in the Leyte campaign, villagers observed him with awe and called him the "White God."

Intensely competitive, Steve moved to Los Angeles to continue his training at both Vic Tanny's and Bert Goodrich's gyms. His mother was a nutritionist, and Steve's dietary knowledge played a large part in his ripped muscularity at a time when anabolic steroids for muscle building were unheard of. His showmanship was not on par with his beauty, and he lost to crack performers Clarence Ross in the 1948 Mr. USA contest and John Grimek in the 1948 Mr. Universe event. In another attempt at the coveted Mr. USA title in 1949, Reeves lost again to both Grimek and Ross. Though he won the Mr. World contest at Cannes, France, that year, he never returned to the American professional bodybuilding arena, but retired, surpassed in competition only by the two American stars.

Reeves's venture into American movies was less memorable. Film director Cecil B. DeMille, overwhelmed by the body of this one-man extravaganza, put Steve on contract. He did a small bit in a B-picture, *Jail Bait*, and had a larger role in the successful film *Athena* (1954). He also did atmosphere work on the Broadway productions of *Kismet* and *The Vamp*, but he was not seen as an acting talent, and his American stage and screen career came to a halt.

While back in Oakland training to be a plumber, Steve received a letter from Italian film producer Pietro Francesi offering him the starring role in *The Labors of Hercules*, to be shot in Italy. Through the film, Reeves's demigod physique became a worldwide sensation. Ironically, film distributor Joseph Levine brought to America the Reeves muscle epics, and Steve thereby achieved star status. Making up to a quarter of a million dollars per picture, he soon became a millionaire.

He married Countess Lina Czarzewicz in 1963. Though now over fifty years old, Steve still keeps much of his former muscularity with steady training. An extremely private person, he has made recent public appearances at bodybuilding functions. He lives with his wife on a ranch near Vista, California, where he raises quarter horses.

Mr. Pacific Coast.

Posing at the 1947 Mr. America contest, which he won.

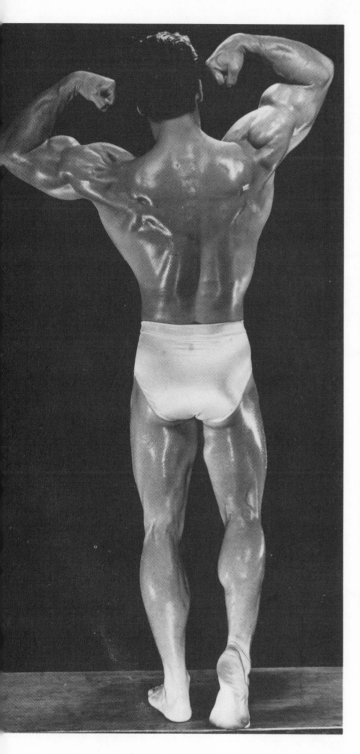

Posing in London at the 1948 Mr. Universe contest.

On the left, Clancy Ross.

With actress Jane Kean.

Reeves in a composite that prefigures the later Mr. Olympia title.

On the set of MGM's production *Athena*, which featured a Mr. Universe contest. Reeves stands behind the barbell to the right of Bert Goodrich, who served as technical director on the film. Number 5, behind Bert to the left, is Irvin Koszewski.

Reeves is number 13; Koszewski kneels at center.

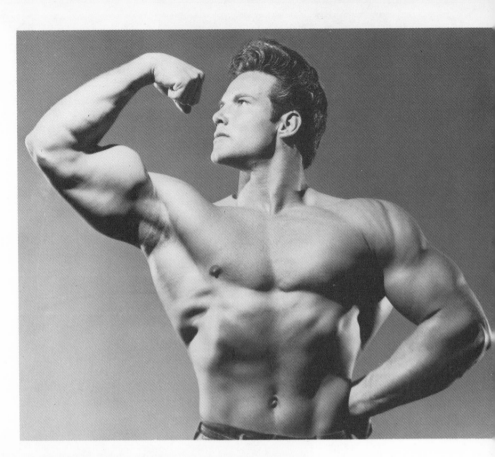

At right, George Eiferman.

Struggling with Primo Carnera, heavyweight boxing champ and a costar in *Hercules Unchained*.

From *Hercules Unchained*.

GEORGE EIFERMAN

To the cognoscenti of bodybuilding George Eiferman was known as "Ingenuous George." His childlike simplicity served a character that was engaging and comical. But it did not in any way belie the terrible intensity of his strength and determination.

Born in Philadelphia, Pennsylvania, in 1925, he inherited his predisposition to massive muscle from his Hungarian ancestors. He started training at age sixteen, using buckets of water and burlap sacks full of produce as weights. He enlisted in the wartime navy, where he continued to train. On returning home in 1946 he joined the well-known Fritche's Gym, where he really began to build the muscle that made him famous.

In 1947 he placed fifth in the Mr. America contest won by Steve Reeves. In 1948 Eiferman won the Mr. America title. He tried for the Professional Mr. USA title in both 1949 and 1950 without success, but twelve years later, in 1962, he proved his durability by winning the IFBB Mr. Universe title. During those interim years he exhibited and lectured year-round at high school assemblies throughout America. His act consisted of a stream of humorous patter, à la Will Rogers, and feats of strength. He could press a young lady sitting on his hand while he played a flawless melody on his trumpet with the other hand. He answered questions on health and training, and it would be safe to say that Eiferman inspired more young people of that era than any other bodybuilder. Auditoriums rocked with laughter at his humor. His answer to the training question "What do you think about breathing, Mr. Eiferman?" was "I think it is very necessary."

He seemed to toy with workouts. He could bench press 300 for ten reps and press 275 behind the head. At 5 feet 7½ inches he weighed 198 in top shape. He had a deep rib box with thick pectorals and short, massive arms. No bodybuilder before or since has been more herculean.

In 1954 Eiferman, with an idea for a muscleman cabaret act, persuaded the fabulous Mae West to come out of retirement. Featuring eight of the nation's top bodybuilders, the show broke box office records throughout America and went on for several years.

Eiferman today is a successful gym operator, with installations in both Vista, California, and Las Vegas, Nevada. He remains big and muscular, and one of his current training partners is none other than his old adversary, Steve Reeves.

At a bodyweight of just over 200 pounds.

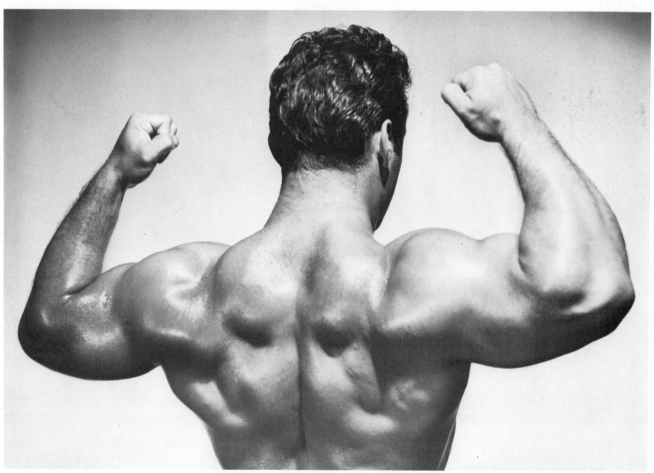

The bodybuilder as youth counselor at a boys' summer camp.

In a conclave of bodymen and admirers. The men are, left to right, in the back row, Armand Tanny, Vince Gironda, and George Eiferman. In the foreground, Alex Aronis and Monte Wolford.

Eiferman and Joe Gold, founder of the world-famous Gold's Gym in Santa Monica, acting in the chorus for Mae West's famous Las Vegas act featuring nine Muscle Beach bodybuilders.

IFBB Mr. Universe 1962.

ARMAND TANNY

Born March 5, 1919, in Rochester, New York, Armand Tanny has applied bodybuilding concepts to his life.

Armand started training at age thirteen under the guidance of his brother, Vic Tanny, who later stirred the nation to fitness with his chain of elaborate gyms. Though Armand excelled at high school sports, weightlifting captivated him. While still in his teens he won an award for being the first man in New York State to clean and jerk 300 pounds. Some years later he was able to clean that amount with one arm.

He moved to California in 1939, where he followed a premedical curriculum at UCLA, and then took up physical therapy training. He continued weightlifting and became Pacific Coast Heavyweight Weightlifting Champion in 1941 with an 840-pound total. A subsequent knee injury sustained while wrestling hampered his progress as a lifter and cut short his enlistment in the coast guard during World War II.

However, Armand continued weight-training without letup, experimenting with different systems, using his knowledge of muscle biomechanics. He watched the emergence of the great physique stars of the era—Ross, Stephan, Eiferman, and Reeves—and at the insistence of his training partners, who saw the results of his seventeen years of weight-training, entered his first physique show in 1949 at thirty years of age. It was Professional Mr. USA, the most talked-about show in bodybuilding history. With six thousand fans screaming for the likes of Grimek, Ross, Reeves, and Eiferman, all former Mr. Americas, and for dark horse Tanny, the contest marked a turning point in show production of muscle. Understandably unable to win, Tanny returned the following year to take the Mr. USA title. In that short year of competition he also won Mr. 1949 and Professional Mr. America in 1950.

He designed weight-training courses for combat crews of the Strategic Air Command. He helped develop the advanced equipment for the Vic Tanny gyms and many of the modern training systems of the Weider Research Group. He has been writing training articles since 1949, and presently, as feature editor of *Muscle Builder* magazine, he writes provocative pieces on training and stories about the stars; he also covers major national and international muscle contests.

Armand Tanny remains in excellent shape today with weight-training, running, bicycling, and skin diving, and stays ahead of the rats in the race with extended vacations in his favorite tropical islands. His home is in Canoga Park, California.

Left to right: George Eiferman, second place Mr. USA 1949; Armand Tanny, first place Mr. USA 1949; and Vic Nicoletti, Mr. Western America 1949.

Bernard McFadden presenting the 1950 Mr. Pro America trophy as Miss Golden Gate looks on.

JACK DELINGER

Jack Delinger's strikingly massive physique became the rage of bodybuilding fans in the late 1940s. It was an era of body types—Ross, Reeves, and Tanny were emerging. Bodybuilding was relatively new, and the ancestral extraction of each new champion—for the most part European—added variety and surprise. Delinger was of Swedish stock.

Although at age eleven Jack suffered an attack of rheumatic fever that nearly destroyed his natural start, he recovered and began to practice handbalancing and gymnastics. He could do two-arm planches, the crucifix on the Roman rings, and one-arm chins. By the time he began high school, he was a powerful handbalancing bottom man and was immediately accepted on the school gymnastics team.

Jack's bodybuilding ability was a product of Ed Yarick's gym in Oakland, California, which spawned many famous stars of the era. Never a skinny kid, he had every natural advantage when he started training at age fifteen. He weighed 150 pounds and had 15-inch arms and 22-inch thighs. The first time he gripped a barbell he pressed 150 pounds.

After two years of bodybuilding training—in the first two months he put on twenty pounds of bodyweight—he entered the Mr. California contest in 1945 and won Best Arms, Chest, and Back and repeated these wins at the Mr. Pacific Coast event. In 1948 Jack beat George Eiferman for the Mr. Western America title, but a few weeks later he lost the Mr. America title to Eiferman. In 1949 Delinger took the Mr. America title, beating the popular Melvin Wells, who won the Most Muscular title.

Jack disappeared from competition for several years, but he retained his impact with great photos in the muscle magazines. He reappeared in 1956 with ultimate mass and muscularity to beat the famous Bill Pearl for the Professional Mr. Universe title at the London Palladium. At his best, Jack weighed 205 at a quoted height of 5 feet, 8½ inches. (He was probably shorter.) He had a 50-inch chest and 31-inch waist.

Jack still lives in Oakland. His last known business venture was operating a gym-equipment sales company.

LÉO ROBERT

French-Canadian Léo Robert rose to fame as a winner of a self-improvement contest in 1947. In the vanguard of a postwar bodybuilding boom, he took advantage of the rapidly developing bodybuilding systems. He first appeared in the "Future Greats" column of my newly launched *Muscle Power* magazine. He had put 2½ inches on his arms and 4½ inches on his chest in a few months of training along lines advocated by that magazine. He won Best Abdominals in his first contest and won that title in every contest he entered thereafter.

Robert had gained 20 pounds to win the self-improvement contest, and photos of his perfectly chiseled muscles and fine proportions immediately immortalized his physique. His body had that rare quality not necessarily found among the greatest bodybuilders—beauty.

At his peak he carried 170 pounds of powerful, perfectly sculpted muscle. His biceps were 16⁴/₅ inches; chest, 47; waist, 30; thighs, 24; and calves, 16. Writer George F. Jowett described him in *Your Physique* magazine in 1948: "Every muscle is perfect in its natural symmetry. They look like block forgings fashioned on the master's anvil and skillfully inserted into the anatomical scheme, welded there with the magic quality of enduring energy."

Robert was as rugged as a rock. He went on to win the contest for Canada's Most Muscular Man. Jowett further clarified his tribute: "If ever there was a monument to progressive bodybuilding and its sensible principles, Léo could be just that. He is an outstanding contribution to intelligent forethought and a determined insistency that goes with it."

Robert ate sensibly and avoided sugars. His chief interests were history, philosophy, hygiene, and physical culture. He loved music, excelling on the trombone, which he played in the army band. He loved hard training. His pet exercises were the bent arm pullover and the bench press. He seriously plotted his progress and stripped it of all fancy. Sober and reserved, he remains a sound embodiment of the old slogan: "A sound mind in a sound body." Robert still lives in Canada.

71

Professional Mr. Universe 1955.

With fellow Canadian Ed Thériault.

ED THÉRIAULT

At a height of 5 feet 1½ inches and weighing 132 pounds, Ed Thériault was considered the world's most perfectly developed short man. His diminutive height and herculean proportions first caught the attention of the bodybuilding world around the end of World War II after decades spent celebrating the muscular giants. He became a mini-giant.

In only four years of training, Thériault proved that a small man with an ordinary start could become a bodybuilding superstar. Born in Canada in 1919, he began training in his teens, experimenting with different methods. At that time I was editor and publisher of *Your Physique* magazine. I recognized Thériault's potential, took him in tow, and showed him proven weight-training methods.

During his three and a half years in the Canadian Army, mostly in Labrador, Thériault continued to train, and his outstanding physique and strength attracted the attention of the command. He was often featured in newspapers and magazines that carried glowing accounts of his amazing physical abilities. His type of strength excited admiration; it was the kind that could demonstrate amazing power in any physical test. He was an expert tumbler and acrobat as well as a superior weightlifter. He came close to the existing Olympic lift records in his class with 200-pound press, 200 snatch, and 260 clean and jerk. He could do a running somersault over three chairs and land like a cat, stand on one hand and hold a 25-pound dumbbell in the other hand, do fifteen tiger-bend press-ups and eighteen handstand dips between chairs.

Thériault's measurements were: arms, 16½ inches; normal chest, 43; waist, $27^{1}/_{10}$; thighs, 22½; and calves, $14^{7}/_{10}$. In proportion to height and weight, he had the largest arm of any known athlete of his time. He gave exhibitions in a black posing cabinet. Earle Liederman, editor of my magazine *Your Physique*, stated: "Thériault, like Sandow and Grimek, can relax and just be himself and still display perfection." A caption from an old photo reads: "No matter from what angle you look at him, the mighty Ed Thériault remains in a class by himself—powerful legs, massive chest, astounding arms, tremendous back—truly a man of super-normal all-around development."

He presently lives in Montreal, Canada.

IRVIN KOSZEWSKI

The measure of a great bodybuilder is his dedication to the game, not only as sport, but also as a way of life. "Zabo," as Koszewski is fondly known, remains something of a landmark in muscledom. Popular, easygoing, and outspoken, he goes on record as never having missed a workout except during the two years he spent in the jungles of New Guinea and the Philippines with the U.S. Army during World War II.

He was born on August 20, 1923, in Camden, New Jersey. He had the natural ruggedness of his Polish ancestry, and in the muscle-conscious world of Camden began weight training while still in grammar school. A superb high school athlete, he became captain of his swimming and wrestling teams and made all-state guard in football for the state of New Jersey.

Koszewski won the Mr. New Jersey title in 1948, and shortly after that went to live in California. Five-hour daily training sessions built his durability into legend. Training partners who tried to work along with him either became anemic or switched to less demanding roles. Sardonic, fun-loving, and noisy, he epitomized all the advantages and drawbacks of cult bodybuilding during that era. He caroused, wenched, smoked, and drank, and yet he never missed a workout: The limits of kicks were carefully defined. He continued to compete, winning such titles as Mr. Los Angeles and Mr. West Coast. Bit parts in movies suited his style, and he had a continuing call for several years on the television series "Combat." He was part of Mae West's cabaret act featuring top musclemen, and he also worked in Jimmy Durante's nightclub act.

At the age of forty-eight he won the Most Muscular title at the 1971 IFBB Mr. America contest. He was invited to exhibit at the 1978 Mr. Heart of America show in St. Louis, Missouri, where at age fifty-five he displayed a muscularity as good as ever without the help of the anabolic drugs in common use today.

His abdominals are famous. It was customary for him to work them daily for half an hour without pause.

Zabo still works in the movies and helps manage the popular World Gym in Santa Monica, California. He never misses his daily workout. He is rock hard, and he eats sparingly. He proves that peak shape and excellent looks can be retained for many years.

Mr. California 1954.

Posed to accentuate his famous
abdominal development.

84

The mature Zabo, still showing all-star form.

REG PARK

Reg Park was born in Leeds, England, on June 7, 1928. He was brought up in a comfortable home, and his physical ability became apparent when he excelled at sports in school, especially rugby and gymnastics. When he was only sixteen years old, he ran the hundred-yard dash in 10.3 seconds. At the time he weighed 174 pounds at 6 feet, a strong hint of his potential for bodybuilding. A year later he won Britain's Perfect Boy contest, and his photos began to appear in muscle magazines.

He went from school into the army and served for a while in Scotland, where his reputation as an athlete and strongman earned him a position as a physical fitness instructor. He was subsequently transferred to Malaya, where he served for eighteen months. From the army he went to Leeds College of Commerce; while he was there he began intensifying his weight training.

At the age of twenty-one Reg Park won the Mr. Britain title at a bodyweight of 220 and height of 6 feet 1 inch. His 18½-inch arm foretold his great potential for muscle mass. He came to the United States and traveled the land for six months, learning American training methods and meeting the top musclemen. Because of his superb development, I featured him prominently in my muscle magazines. His popularity soared, and he became known throughout the bodybuilding world.

With a world-caliber physique by this time, he appeared unbeatable, but in the same era that superb bodybuilder from California, Steve Reeves, was at large. Both competed for the 1950 Mr. Universe title, and Reeves won. It was Park's only defeat in that period.

Park was bigger the following year, 1951, at 225 pounds and chest 53½ inches, and better: He won a popular decision for the Mr. Universe title. In 1958 he won the title again. Seven years after that, in 1965, he won the Professional Mr. Universe title and became the first triple winner in history. In 1970, twenty years after his big battle with Reeves, Reg met the upcoming young Arnold Schwarzenegger and lost the Professional Mr. Universe title to the incredibly muscled newcomer.

After successful physical-culture business ventures in England, Reg moved to South Africa, where he now conducts his successful gym business. He married South African ballerina Marean Isaacs, sister of John Isaacs, a former Mr. Universe class winner. At age 50+ he still retains a fair degree of the mass and muscularity that almost thirty years ago set a new trend in muscular development. He makes occasional appearances today as a master of ceremonies for major world contests.

Park as he appeared at the 1970 Professional Mr. Universe contest, which he lost to Arnold Schwarzenegger.

BILL PEARL

In 1953 Bill Pearl soared to national prominence in bodybuilding by capturing the Mr. America title. He won the Mr. Universe title in London that same year. At twenty-two years of age, this fine athlete, equipped with nearly perfect proportions, had begun a career in competitive bodybuilding that stretched through eighteen years, remarkable not only as the longest career, but also for his world class competition victories.

Born in Pineville, Oregon, in 1930, Bill began training at an early age and became a fine all-around athlete, excelling at wrestling. He joined the navy, and while stationed in San Diego, California, became the naval district wrestling champion there. It was also there that he met his lifelong friend and business associate Leo Stern, a San Diego gym operator, who coached him through all of his professional victories. As the Mr. America titlist, Bill did valuable public relations work for the navy and received special commendations.

Inspired by two superstars of the time, John Grimek and Clancy Ross, Bill went on to win the Mr. Universe title four times, all in London—the second time in 1961, the third in 1967, and the fourth in 1971. In his final victory he was the biggest man who ever won an international title, massive and ripped at 237 bodyweight. He was also forty-one years of age. In that final contest he defeated the world's greatest: Reg Park, Sergio Oliva, and Frank Zane. A defeat by Jack Delinger in 1956 was his only major reverse. However, that same year Bill won the Mr. USA title over the great Clancy Ross.

Bill possessed fine natural proportions and muscular shape, and he never failed to improve with each victory. His posing was superb, and some of his most outstanding photos were deliberate, relaxed shots, artful departures from the usual flexed fare served up in bodybuilding. He also performed an exquisite imitation of Eugene Sandow's act.

He was a physical training consultant for several years with the aerospace program, working mainly to keep the administrative brains in good health.

After leaving the navy, Bill opened his first gym in Sacramento, California. He loved teaching, especially when his students were youngsters. He expanded the business until he had a chain of seven gyms, but then eventually reduced it to his single, presently highly successful installation in Pasadena, California.

Bill has recently been appointed head of the Professional Judges Committee of the IFBB, to which he lends his considerable prestige and experience.

Presently forty-nine years old, he continues to train and give exhibitions. He would still be the toughest competition for the best in the game today.

Mr. America and Mr. Universe
of 1953 at a bodyweight of 210
pounds.

The Mr. Southern California 1953 contest winners. Left to right: Seymour Koenig, third place; Bill Pearl, first place; and Irvin Koszewski, second place.

Bill Pearl, Mr. California 1953, with second-place winner, Irvin Koszewski.

Being congratulated by television actress Jeff Donnell for 1956 Mr. USA victory.

Tearing a license plate in half as part of his strongman act.

Looking on with George Eiferman as a staff member demonstrates equipment at one of Pearl's gyms.

Bill Pearl in form for the 1971 Professional
Mr. Universe contest.

Guest posing at the 1978 Mr. Olympia contest.

CHUCK SIPES

Chuck Sipes was born August 22, 1932, in Sterling, Illinois. While in high school he participated in football, basketball, baseball, and track. He started training with weights in his own home at age sixteen.

He continued his bodybuilding training for many years, constantly revising and improving his routines. After ten years of this he won the 1959 Mr. America title. He followed that up with the Mr. Universe 1961 and the Mr. World 1967 titles. At peak condition he weighed 220 pounds at 5 feet, 9½ inches. His measurements were: arms, 19½ inches; chest, 50; thighs, 25½; calves, 18; and waist, 32. He was particularly known for his massive, powerful forearms, which measured 18 inches.

Sipes was also enormously strong. He could bench press 570 pounds, squat 600, and curl 250. He at one time put together a strongman act in which he blew up a hot water bottle, broke chains, bent iron bars, and tore apart license plates.

Showing the humanitarian spirit often found in men of muscle, Chuck began working with the physically and mentally handicapped. He lectured in schools, churches, colleges, and service academies, promoting fitness and recreation. For the past sixteen years he has been in correctional work with the state of California at the Preston School of Industry.

He is an outdoorsman who began his affair with the wilderness as a lumberjack. He is an active mountaineer and member of the prestigious American Alpine Club. And he is also a western painter of considerable talent.

Chuck Sipes currently lives in California with his wife and three daughters.

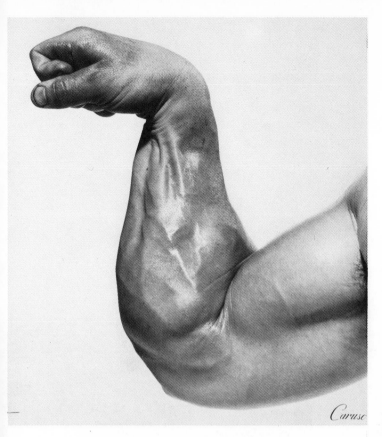

The famous Sipes forearm.

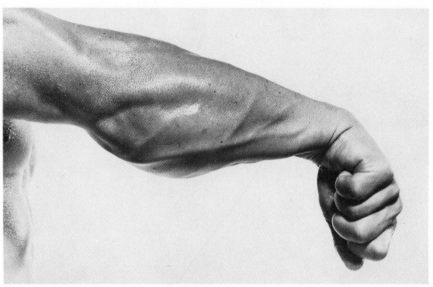

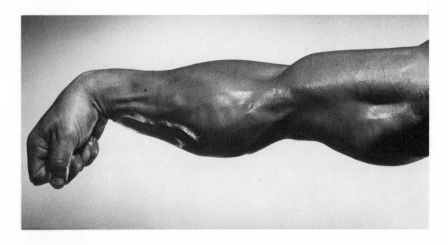

110

112

Bodybuilding's ambassador to the young.

With IFBB President Ben Weider at the 1970 Mr. Asia competition in Singapore.
(The winner is Japan's Mr. Miyamoto.)

LARRY SCOTT

The appearance of Larry Scott truly stimulated the idolatry gland of bodybuilding fans of the middle 1960s. He had the clean-cut good looks of the boy down the street, with the sunny disposition of a summer sky. Add to that a perfectly muscled body built by his own training genius from a 120-pound adolescent frame of no consequence, and you have the makings of a star. He was to bodybuilding what the Beatles were to rock music. The delirium accompanying his exhibits, particularly in hero-conscious New York City, is still remembered.

Born in Blackfoot, Idaho, on November 12, 1938, Larry grew up rather small for most sports until he went to high school, where he practiced on the trampoline. He started weight training at the Pocatello YMCA at age sixteen and four years later won the Mr. Idaho title.

It was always a mystery to Scott's training partners that he would develop muscle and they wouldn't, even though they were doing exactly the same things. As a bodybuilder, he had a strong sense of self-motivation from the moment he happened to pick up a muscle magazine in Pocatello's city dump and read, "You, Too, Can Have an Arm Like This in 30 Days."

He moved to Los Angeles to study electronics and continued his training, first at Bert Goodrich's gym and then at Vince's Gym. He won the Mr. California competition in 1960 at 170 bodyweight. Bigger victories followed: Mr. Pacific Coast, Mr. America in 1962, Mr. Universe in 1964, and finally Mr. Olympia in both 1965 and 1966. He weighed 205 at his peak.

After that, Scott became active in Morman church affairs and abandoned high-powered bodybuilding for several years, during which time his weight slipped to 156 pounds. He eventually returned to the gym for casual training. He moved his family to Salt Lake City, Utah, in 1972 and began giving lectures and exhibitions for the Mormon church, which is enthusiastic about physical culture.

Inspired by invitations to pose at more recent shows, Scott has resumed full-bore training. The exploding popularity of bodybuilding, for which he was a prime catalyst many years ago, plus the sport's growing profit potential, have led him back into the game at forty years of age.

He continues to work in the insurance business in Salt Lake City, where he lives with his wife and five children.

116

Mr. Olympia 1965.

Hamming it up with Ron Teufel, Mr. USA.

With Freddy Ortiz, rival for reputation as the man with the world's best-developed arms.

Mr. Olympia training the next generation of bodymen. 121

SERGIO OLIVA

Sergio Oliva was born in Cuba on July 4, 1941. His early involvement with weights was as a strength athlete. He made a total of 885 on the Olympic lifts at a bodyweight of 198 pounds. He went to Jamaica with the Cuban weightlifting team in 1962 to compete in the Central American Games. With the political storm brewing between Cuba and the United States, Oliva defected, eventually emigrating to America. He made his way to Chicago, where he became a television repairman.

With the new, improved living and training conditions in the Windy City, he grew bigger and stronger, and his body took on phenomenal proportions. He lost interest in Olympic weightlifting and switched to the power lifts. By 1965 he had bench pressed 425 pounds, deadlifted 600, and squatted with 575. Oliva was attracted to the latter movements because of their muscle development potential. Eventually his arms reached 21 inches, with other bodyparts increasing proportionately. His waist remained at 30 inches, and the effect of his massive torso and legs connected by a wasp waist was exaggerated and spectacular.

In 1966 Oliva entered and won the Junior Mr. America title, an AAU-sanctioned event. A short time later he competed in the Senior Mr. America contest and lost to the same bodybuilder, Bob Gajda, he had beaten at the Junior show. On that note Oliva changed his affiliation to the IFBB and began his legendary career as a professional. In 1967 he won the prestigious Mr. Olympia title, topping the very popular stars Dave Draper, Harold Poole, and Chuck Sipes. He won again in 1968 and 1969.

He lost the Mr. Olympia title to the young Austrian, Arnold Schwarzenegger, in 1970. Sergio's reign was over. Shortly thereafter he was defeated for the Mr. Universe title by forty-year-old Bill Pearl. More recently he has attempted comebacks with minimal success, losing to competitors beneath his potential, most likely because he has disregarded the highly ripped, vascular trend of the late 1970s. He depended rather on his natural muscular mass, with which detail was lost and the chance to reign supreme as well.

When Schwarzenegger, six times Mr. Olympia (1970–75), was asked who he thought could ever defeat him, he replied, "Sergio Oliva, in top shape."

IFBB Mr. World 1967.

124

Mr. International 1973, with promoter Eddy Silvestre (left) and Franco Columbu (right), not a featured competitor, but awarded a trophy for a pose-down prompted by an Oliva challenge.

Pumping up with Arnold Schwarzenegger.

127

Guest posing at the 1971 IFBB Mr. Universe contest.

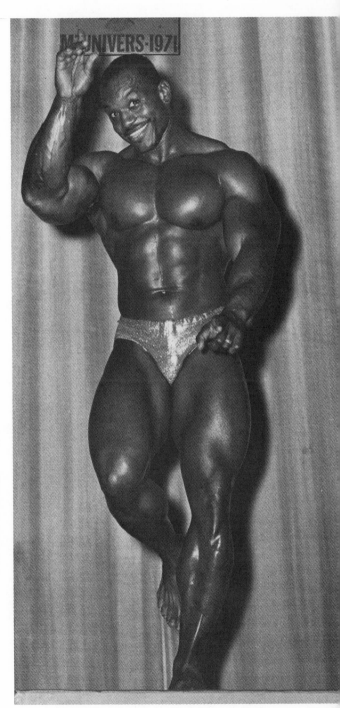

The shirtsleeves are specially tailored to the Oliva arm.

SERGE NUBRET

The islands of the Caribbean have produced several bodybuilding stars. The most notable and perhaps most controversial is Serge Nubret, who was born in Guadeloupe on October 12, 1939. When he was fifteen years old, his land-holding, well-to-do parents sent him to a Paris prep school. There Serge discovered athletics and became an outstanding sprinter and shot-putter. He ran 100 meters in 10.5 seconds.

His track coach introduced him to weight training, and in 1958, after only four months' training, Serge became Mr. Guadeloupe. At the 1959 IFBB Mr. Universe event, he won the Most Muscular Man title. Nubret dropped from competition for a while to study accounting in Paris, but after getting his degree he opened his own gym. He also resumed competition in 1966 and won the Mr. Europe title. More recently, in 1976 he won the National Amateur Body Building Association (NABBA) Professional Mr. Universe title and in 1977 the World Amateur Body Building Association (WBBA) Mr. World prize. In Pretoria, South Africa, in 1975, he placed second to the insuperable Arnold Schwarzenegger in the Mr. Olympia competition.

At 5 feet 11 inches, Nubret maintains a competition weight of 212 pounds. His arm recently measured 21½ inches pumped. Tremendously strong, he has bench pressed 508 pounds at 220 bodyweight.

He presently owns two gyms in Paris, one for men and one for women, gives exhibitions throughout the world, and is chief administrator of his new bodybuilding organization.

He has had an extensive career as an actor in thirty films. During the period when the Hercules films were popular European productions, Nubret made a picture called *Son of Hercules*, a parody of the classic image. He also played in a German television series version of *Huckleberry Finn*.

Today at forty years of age Nubret remains one of the most intensely muscular men in competition. He has superb proportions and perfectly chiseled bodyparts.

His astounding performance on stage in the apartheid climate of South Africa in the 1975 Mr. Olympia contest gave pause for thought: With racial barriers lowered there for bodybuilding, other racial barriers could follow.

IFBB Mr. Europe 1971.

Competing with Franco
Columbu for the IFBB Mr.
Universe title.

At the 1975 Mr. Olympia competition in South Africa.

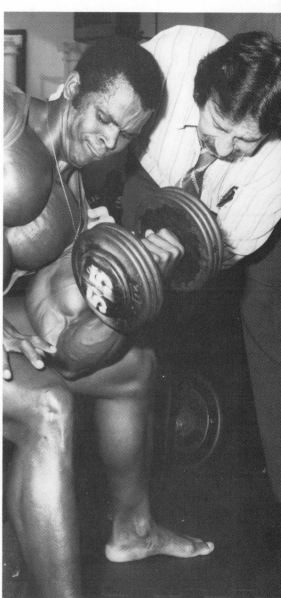

Nubret concentrates on a Weider training tip.

ED CORNEY

Ed Corney was born in Honolulu, Hawaii, in 1933. Considered to be the best poser since Sandow, the charismatic Corney had no desire to be a competitive bodybuilder and was entirely unheard of until he was thirty-six years old.

His Hawaiian heritage and a rugged life on the tropical islands gave him a head start. Following a four-year stint in the coast guard, he settled in the city of Fremont, California. Inspired by two muscle stars of that era, Alan Stephan and Jack Delinger, he started weight training at the age of twenty-six.

He trained for ten years before he entered and won his first contest, Mr. Fremont. Taken by all the attention and the fascination of contest training, he went on to win all the regional titles, including Mr. West Coast. In 1971 Ed won his height class in the IFBB Mr. America contest and also the Mr. USA title, overall, a milestone in competitive bodybuilding for a short-class competitor in international events; proving that a good small man could beat a good big man. In 1972 he won the overall IFBB Mr. America title.

Ed believes that every great bodybuilding success is marked by a year of consummate effort involving absolute adherence to diet and three hours of daily training. It never happens the same way twice. The crowning year for him was 1972, when he was acclaimed Mr. Universe in Baghdad, Iraq, the overall title. He had again proved that perfection could win over size. He did not reach this peak shape again, even though he won somewhat lesser titles the following two years—best of his height class in the Mr. World and Mr. International events. He has entered the Mr. Olympia contest several times since then without winning, but his posing has been a highlight of every show.

Corney combines fluid grace with absolute muscle control and timing. His moves are functional and pleasing. Arnold Schwarzenegger best describes it: "Corney sets a mood for the audience, arouses something dormant in them that doesn't surface until he starts moving—then he turns them on."

The picture on the cover of the famous best seller *Pumping Iron* is of Ed Corney. As he describes it, "I have both my arms flung up in an expression of joy. It conveys what I feel, that bodybuilding is a joyous, exciting, healthful, magnificent adventure."

M. UNIVERS·1971

A master poser holds the attention of fellow
competitors at the 1971 IFBB Mr. Universe
contest.

Joe Weider congratulates IFBB Mr. America 1972.

IFBB Professional Mr. Universe 1975.

Posing against Bill Grant and
Bill Mitchell at the 1974 Mr.
World competition held in
Madision Square Garden's Felt
Forum. The title went to Grant
(left).

At the 1975 Mr. Olympia contest in South
Africa.

Posing at the 1977 Mr. Olympia contest.

ARNOLD SCHWARZENEGGER

Arnold Schwarzenegger was born in Graz, Austria, July 30, 1947. His father was a sports-minded police inspector, and Arnold was brought up in a tradition of strength. By the time he was seventeen years old he had won the Junior Mr. Austria contest and also the Junior Styrian Weightlifting Championship with a 705-pound total. At age 20 he won the Mr. Universe title.

I spotted Arnold in Europe and brought him to America on a long-term contract. Personable and ambitious, he learned English, and with professional guidance and constant magazine exposure, he marketed his very profitable bodybuilding courses. He also pursued an extensive curriculum in business administration at UCLA.

He trained in the lively bodybuilding mecca of Santa Monica, California, cheered on by his many worshippers, and he still lives and conducts many of his business ventures in that oceanside city.

In 1970 Arnold began toppling in competition the very people who had first inspired him. In the Mr. Universe event he beat his idol, Reg Park. In the Mr. World contest he defeated Sergio Oliva, Boyer Coe, Dave Draper, Franco Columbu, and Dennis Tinerino. At the Mr. Olympia competition that year Arnold again defeated the seemingly insuperable Oliva, and began a five-year onslaught that ended with retirement after six consecutive Mr. Olympia victories.

He has sought the logical outlet for an exhibition sport, motion pictures, and has starred in two critically acclaimed features, *Stay Hungry* and *Pumping Iron*. He is presently contracted for a series of *Conan* features, a role suitably barbaric for the affable, bold, massive, aggressive man his friends have dubbed "the Austrian Oak." At 6 feet 2 inches he weighs 230 pounds, with arms, 22; chest, 57; waist, 32; thighs, 28; calves, 18. He has become a popular guest on many of the nation's television talk shows.

Together with attorney Jim Lorimer, Arnold has promoted the highly successful and exciting IFBB-sanctioned Mr. Olympia shows at Columbus, Ohio, since his retirement from the sport in 1975.

Schwarzenegger's vaulting bodybuilding success came at a time when the world began to take greater cognizance of individual effort in sport. This champion was the visual embodiment of the human desire to excel. He wore his massive muscle like a badge. He trained openly and purposefully for all to see. He proselytized and pumped. He showed his compatriots and the world that bodybuilding could be profitable. "I have made it in my mail-order business, real estate, and films," he tells them. "I am a hunter. One has to hunt for it, each in his own way."

Congratulating Sergio Oliva on
the latter's Mr. Olympia victory
in 1969. Joe Weider looks on.

Arnold does donkey toe raises with Franco Columbu, Frank Zane, and Pete Caputo astride his back.

Arnold the gladiator, star of the low-budget film *Hercules in New York* (1970).

At the 1970 AAU Professional Mr. World competition. Sergio Oliva (left) and Dennis Tinerino (right).

Mr. Olympia 1971 receives congratulations from Serge Nubret and Joe Weider.

The champions pose for the judges at the 1972 Mr. Olympia. Top, left to right: Sergio Oliva, Arnold Schwarzenegger, Serge Nubret, and Frank Zane. Bottom, left to right: Franco Columbu, Sergio Oliva, Arnold Schwarzenegger, Serge Nubret, and Frank Zane.

Mr. Olympia 1973.

With Lou Ferrigno at the 1974 Mr. Olympia.

Mr. Olympia 1974.

Schwarzenegger and Columbu, the first of the bodybuilders to undertake a dual posing routine.

Arnold with Ed Corney, training partner for the 1975 Mr. Olympia contest.

Check posing. Arnold and Franco consider training progress.

Training for the 1975 Mr. Olympia. Looking on at left is Denny Gable.

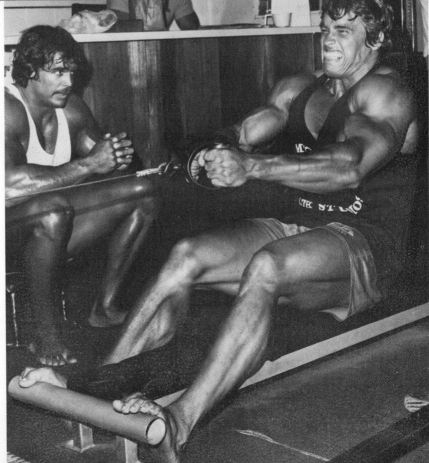

As promoter of the 1976 Mr. Olympia contest, with Ben Weider, IFBB President.

Joking with Racquel Welch at the 1977 Golden Globe awards.

Checking out Franco's new bike.

FRANCO COLUMBU

Franco Columbu was born in Sardinia on August 7, 1941. His parents were in the horse riding business, and when Franco was ten years old he won an award for artistic riding. He also tended the neighbors' sheep and goats and had to climb and run in the steep mountains for hours every day. This exercise gave him enormous leg power and endurance at an early age.

With so much stamina, Franco turned to boxing for a living. He scored thirty consecutive knockouts. While fighting in Germany he met Arnold Schwarzenegger in a Munich gym, and the two became fast friends. The clang of weights became Franco's song, and he gave up boxing to drive a taxi and lift weights. He won the German Powerlifting Championship in 1968 with 1650 pounds total for the bench press, squat, and deadlift. He is only 5 feet 3 inches tall, and it is said that the doormen at the meet, unimpressed, at first refused to believe he was a powerlifter and wouldn't let him in.

The mighty little Sardinian went on to win the Mr. Italy title in 1968, as well as the powerlifting title in his weight class. From there he began to savage the iron game. Returning to Munich, he won the Mr. Europe title and the International Powerlifting Contest, held jointly, with a total of 1700 pounds. Shortly thereafter he placed second in the London Mr. Universe competition in his class and also won the Mr. Western Europe title in Belgium. Then, along with his companion Arnold, he left for America, the hotbed of bodybuilding.

Neither man lost any time in the land of opportunity. They trained together until separated by their respective studies in 1973, Arnold pursuing business administration and Franco chiropractic. Franco was graduated from the Cleveland School of Chiropractic and now shares a successful practice with his wife, Anita, also a doctor of chiropractic.

Franco pursued the Mr. Olympia title, which friend Schwarzenegger captured year after year until 1975. Finally in 1976, after Arnold's retirement, Franco won Mr. Olympia, defeating Frank Zane, his toughest competition that year.

During the shooting of a television strongman special the following summer, Franco was gravely injured and underwent extensive knee surgery. He returned to training to give posing exhibitions, but has neither lifted nor competed since.

Truly one of the world's great strongmen, Franco has done a 475-pound bench press, 655 squat, and 735 deadlift. On the Olympic lifts he has pressed 350, snatched 290, and cleaned and jerked 365. In his top shape at 188 bodyweight with chest 52 inches, arms 19, and waist 29½, Franco had diamond-hard muscularity. Extremely popular throughout the world, he continues to be one of the most widely traveled bodybuilding performers.

The European champion.

Receiving the 1970 Mr. Europe trophy from IFBB President Ben Weider.

Posing with Frank Zane at the 1974 Mr. Olympia.

Preparing for a photography
session with Jimmy Caruso.

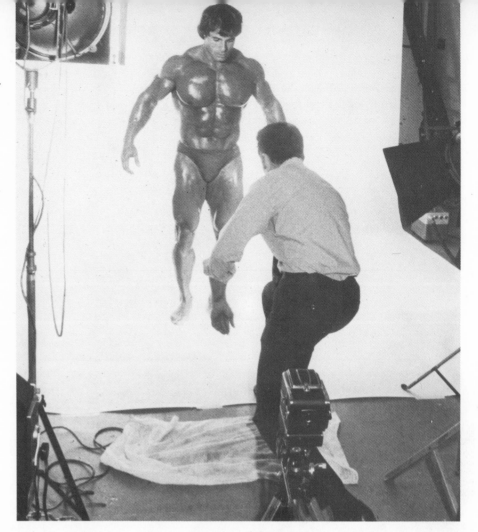

Class winner (under 200 pounds) at the 1975 Mr. Olympia. The runners-up: Ed Corney (left) and Albert
Beckles of England (right).

Caruso

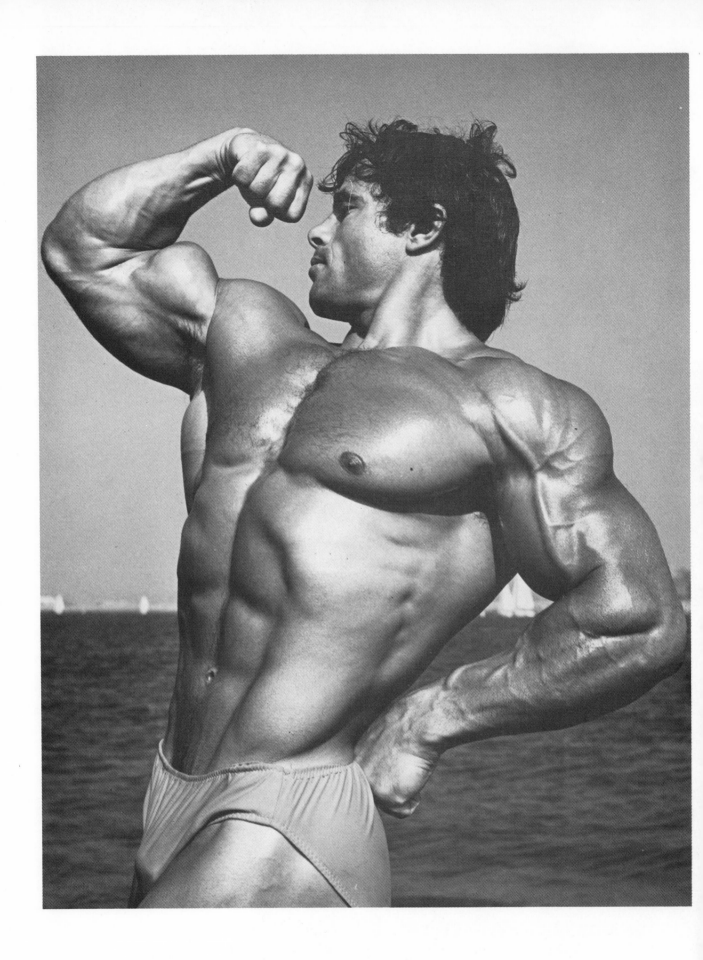

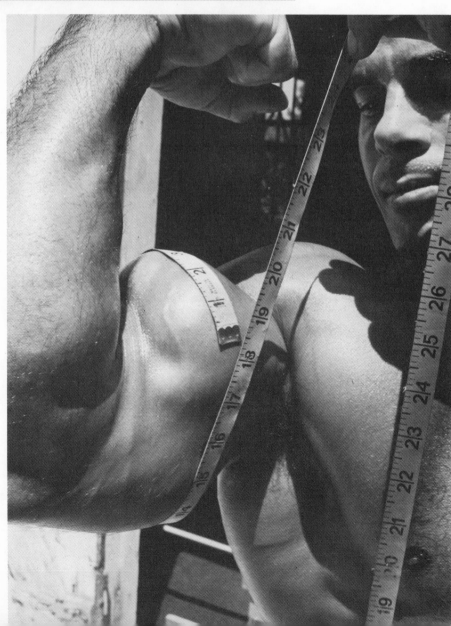

Training at his home gym.

A moment at ease with Joe Weider.

With wife, Anita, accepting the formal declaration of American Bodybuilding Week from Los Angeles Mayor Tom Bradley, July 1977.

177

Glimpses of the Columbu strongman act.

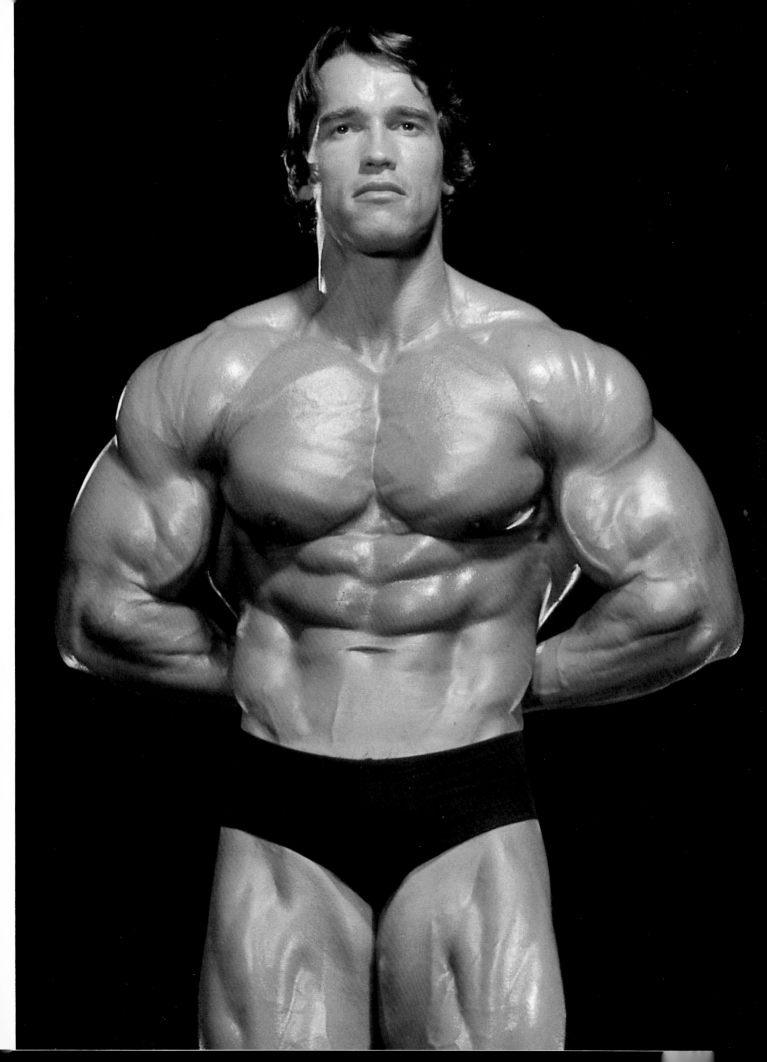

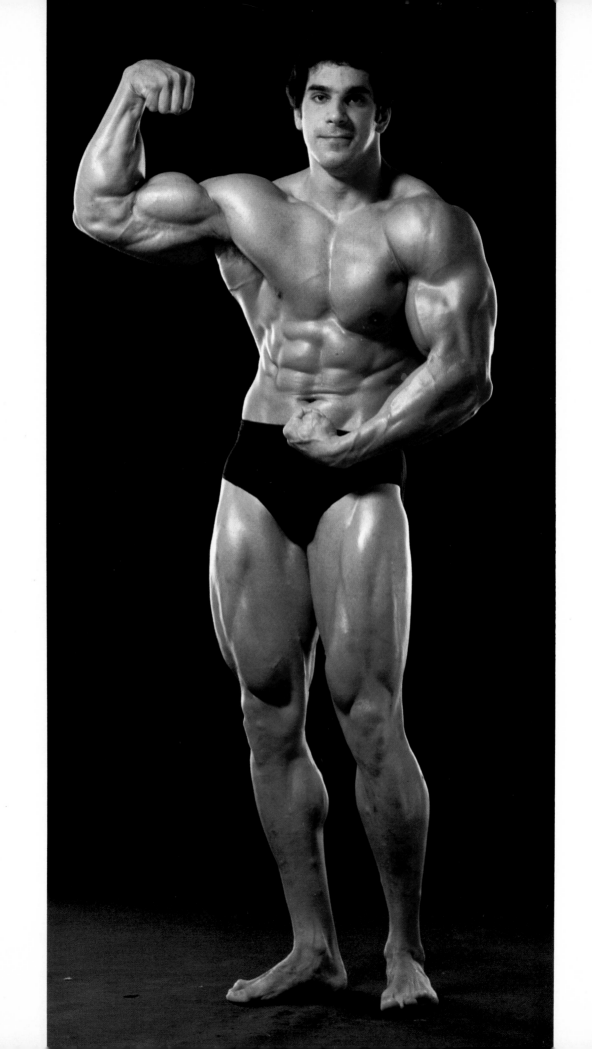

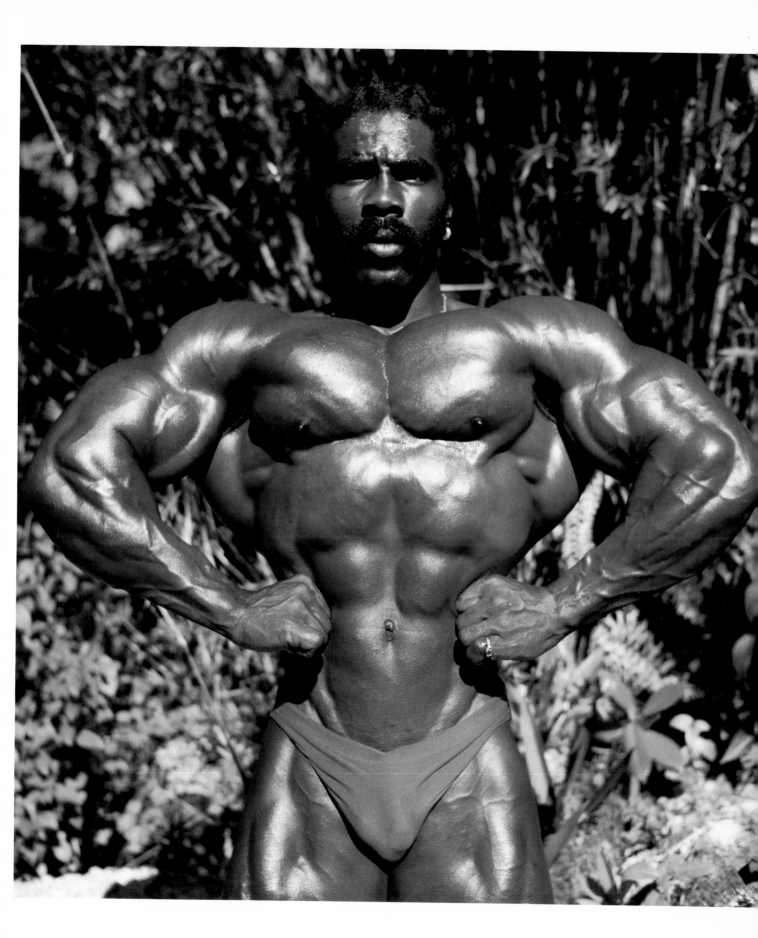

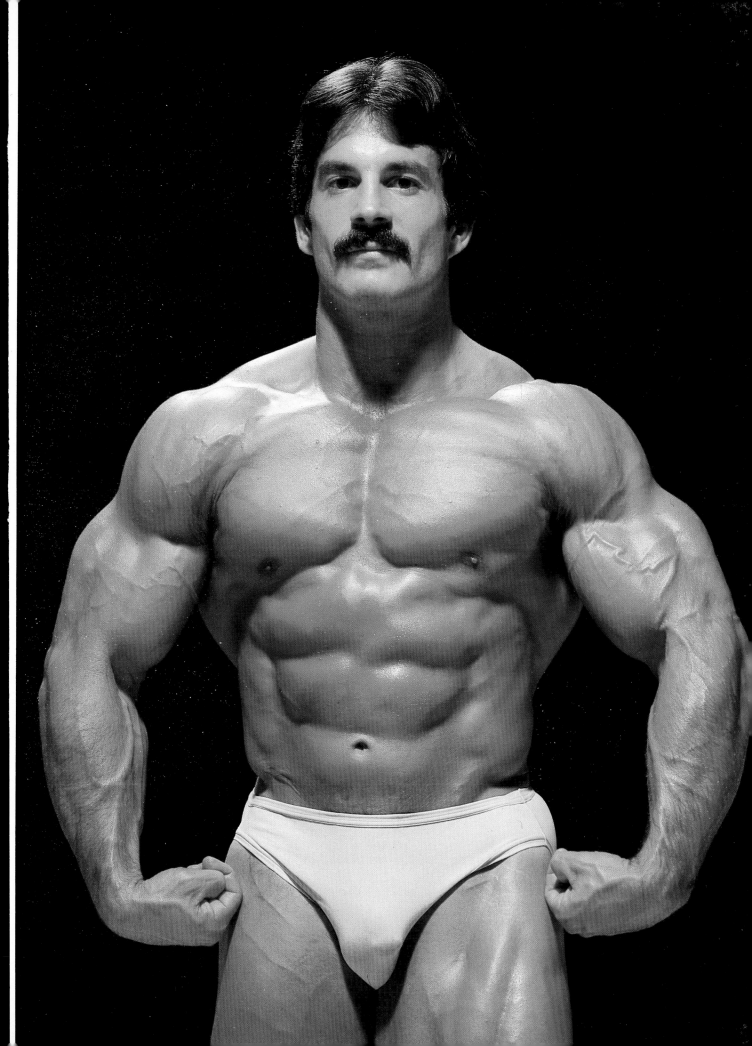

DANNY PADILLA

ROBBY ROBINSON

DANNY PADILLA

ROBBY ROBINSON / DANNY PADILLA

ROBBY ROBINSON

ROBBY ROBINSON / DANNY PADILLA

DANNY PADILLA

ROBBY ROBINSON

DANNY PADILLA

ROBBY ROBINSON

Robby Robinson was born in Tallahassee, Florida. He began weight training with primitive equipment. As a competitive lifter he pressed 300 pounds and did 500-pound squats and 900-pound leg presses in training. He trained for a considerable time before ever seeing a bodybuilding magazine. Then *Muscle Builder*, with its excellent physique photos and training articles, became his staple-bound coach. With the wide shoulders and narrow waist typical of his race, he had phenomenal potential for growth. The editors of *Muscle Builder* once taped his arm at 21½ cold and his waist at 27½.

When Robby saw Sergio Oliva win the 1967 Mr. Olympia event, he converted to all-out bodybuilding. By 1975 he had won, repeatedly, all the main AAU physique contests throughout the southern United States. Then Arnold Schwarzenegger saw him and convinced him to go to California. Just as I had first spotted Arnold in Europe and signed him to a contract, I also saw the Robinson potential and put this black star on my Woodland Hills payroll. There he trains and lends himself to advertising for Weider training equipment and food supplements.

While still in Florida, Robby played football for Florida A & M and was elected to the All-Southern Conference. A superb athlete, he ran the 100-meter in 9.4 seconds.

Though of a quiet nature, Robby promotes an image of flamboyance with his gold front tooth, earring, ethnic hairdos, and colorful clothes. His bodybuilding courses, exhibitions, seminars and contest prizes have made him wealthy, and he lives with his wife, Elaine, in a beautiful pad by the sea in Venice, California.

In both 1977 and 1978 Robby placed second to Frank Zane in the Mr. Olympia contest. A tireless competitor, he trains and grows more massive and cut-up each year, weighing as much as 220 pounds at 5 feet 7½ inches. He trains for ultimate muscular detail, resorting to moderate weights and a variety of movements, never pausing during his fast-paced workouts.

Gracious and grateful for his success, Robby never forgets that he arrived in Los Angeles from Tallahassee with but twenty-five dollars to his name. The near-empty refrigerator he swore would one day be loaded is packed today, but diet-conscious Robby now laughs at the irony: "I can only sit and stare at it."

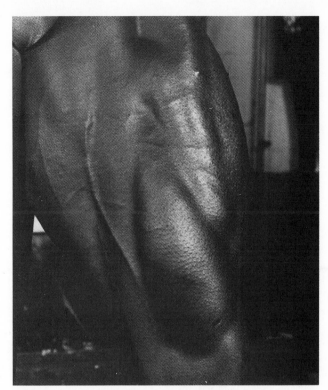

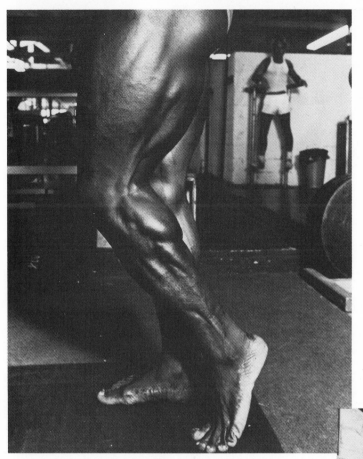

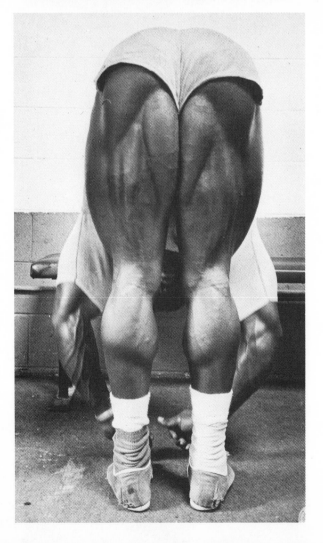

Check posing after a gym workout.

185

Guest posing at the 1977 Mr. America contest in Los Angeles.

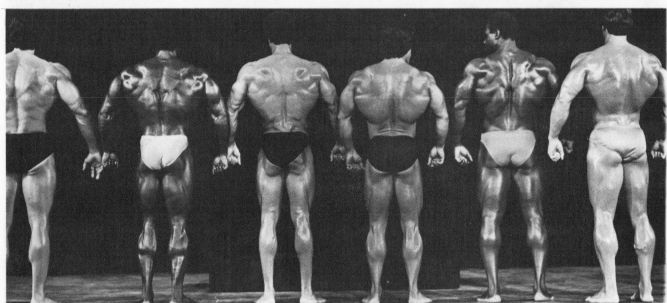

Night of the Champions, New York City, 1978. Left to right: top, Boyer Coe, Bill Grant, Ed Corney, Robby Robinson, Roy Callender, Dennis Tinerino, and Joe Nazario: middle, Tinerino, Robinson, Grant, Corney, Callender, and Coe: bottom, Grant, Tinerino, Corney, Coe, Callender, Robinson.

Winner of the 1978 World Cup. Danny Padilla (left) and Roy Callender (right).

Check posing with Lou Ferrigno.

Moments at ease. With Joe Weider (above) and with wife, Elaine "Sunny" Robinson (below).

Wearing the famous training shirt bought by a fan for $50.

LOU FERRIGNO

At 270 pounds and standing 6 feet 5 inches, Lou Ferrigno, for pure size, has no peer in the bodybuilding world. With 23-inch arms and a 34-inch waist, his structure, proportion, and muscularity come close to perfection. The superhuman image is awesome to behold. He has been the star of the spectacular television series, "The Incredible Hulk," in which his truly incredible physique has been seen by millions of astounded American television viewers.

Lou's big ambition has always been to win the world's top body-building title, Mr. Olympia. Fate boosted him instead to motion picture fame. The movie industry got its first glimpse of Lou when he competed in the "Superstars Competition," a 1976 spectacular television get-together of top athletes from many sports in which he proved himself to be a superb all-around athlete, taking away $14,000 in prize money.

When barely out of infancy, Lou lost his hearing from an ear infection. His father, Matt, a New York police lieutenant, refused to put the quiet child in a school for the deaf, instead providing him with lip-reading lessons. This, along with a classroom front seat, got Lou through school with excellent grades.

Matt Ferrigno, who had a 19-inch arm from weight training, inspired his skinny 6-foot tall, 130-pound son to take up weight training. In a few short years, Lou went on to win the Teen-age Mr. America and Mr. America titles, and he twice won the Mr. Universe title. For a while he worked in the lucrative sheet-metal business, but the urge to compete was so strong that he moved to California in the mid-1970s to train with the super bodybuilders who congregated there in Venice and Santa Monica.

With his sights on the Mr. Olympia title, Lou took his only shot at it in 1975 in South Africa, but lost to the invincible Arnold Schwarzenegger. Lou has continued to train hard, hoping to compete in the Olympia event again, but ever-growing motion picture commitments have snatched him away from the bodybuilding arena. The "Hulk" character forces Lou to maintain his mighty muscularity, and he remains a charter member of the modern muscle community. He currently lives in Santa Monica, where he trains at the well-known World Gym.

Mr. International 1974.

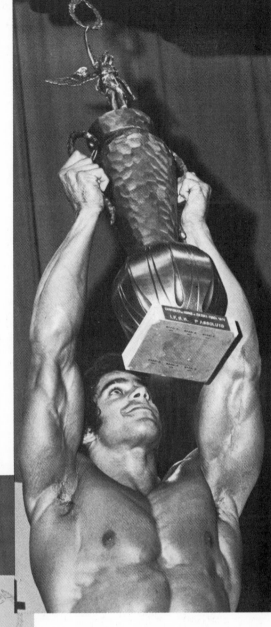

Mr. Universe holding one of his trophies aloft with evident satisfaction.

Mr. Universe 1974. The runners-up are Belgium's Pierre van der Steen (left) and Turkey's Ahmet Enulu (right).

With Joe Weider and Arnold Schwarzenegger at the 1974 Mr. Olympia.

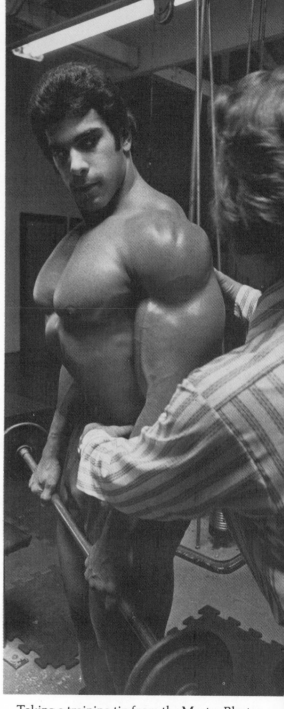

Taking a training tip from the Master Blaster.

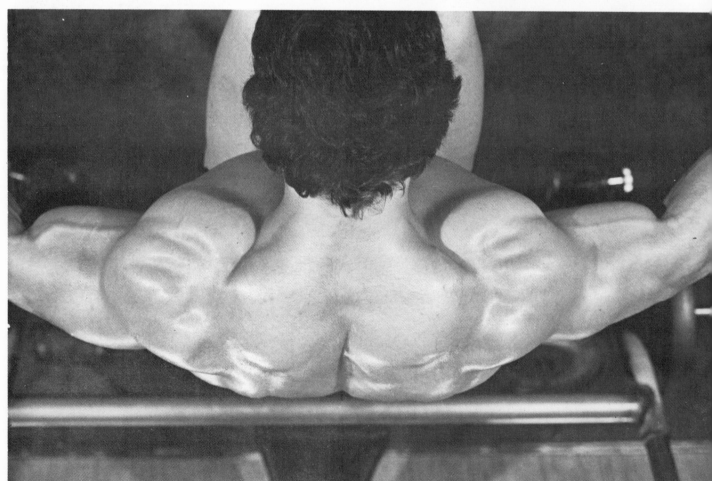

With Reggie Jackson (left) and Ken Norton (middle) on ABC Television's "Superstars" competition.

Assuming the persona of "the Hulk."

FRANK ZANE

The Zane odyssey is a history of wins and losses culminating finally in Frank's Mr. Olympia victories in 1977 and 1978. His career is all the more remarkable for his persistence. It has been a moral crucible, a quest for all-around perfection as much as a desire to be judged a champion.

In 1968, after ten years of training, he won the IFBB Mr. America and Mr. Universe titles. He defeated newcomer Arnold Schwarzenegger. In 1969 he took the IFBB Mr. World and the 1970 NABBA Amateur Mr. Universe titles, and in 1972 the NABBA Professional Mr. Universe titles.

Frank Zane's losses were also many, and it was only after five tries that he finally won the Mr. Olympia contest. He struggled through the years 1970–75 when Arnold held the Mr. Olympia title. In 1976 Zane lost a decision to Franco Columbu by a single point. This only served to fire up his grim determination.

Although highly competitive, Zane considers titles the small rewards for the long, continuing quest for perfection. Faced always with the fight for greater muscle mass, Zane has never considered bodyweight an indication of his condition. He had stopped trying to compete with the naturally more massive bodybuilders on their own terms. "I don't like to create mental battles for myself," he has said, "so I forget about bodyweight. The composite picture at contest time is all that counts." Asked why he continued to compete at the age of thirty-five, he says, "I think for the fans who write and inspire me." The eternal positivist, Zane reasons, "I alone will determine what I will do for myself. I know how to train my body. If I panic about competition, I might overtrain. I do exactly what I have to do, nothing more."

Zane and his wife, Christine, both former teachers, now have devoted themselves entirely to bodybuilding as a profession—writing books, exhibiting, and giving training seminars. Christine herself has won the Miss Americana and Miss Universe Bikini titles. They live in Santa Monica.

Zane's proportions, shape, and definition are hardly less than perfect. A masterful poser, with his bodyweight in the 180s, he presents a classic bodybuilding image.

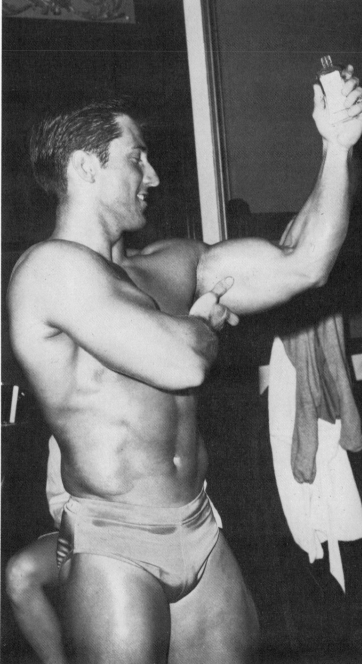

Oiling up.

Mr. America 1969.

Receiving the class winner's award for the 1969
IFBB Mr. World competition from Arnold
Schwarzenegger.

Mr. Universe title winner, 1969.

203

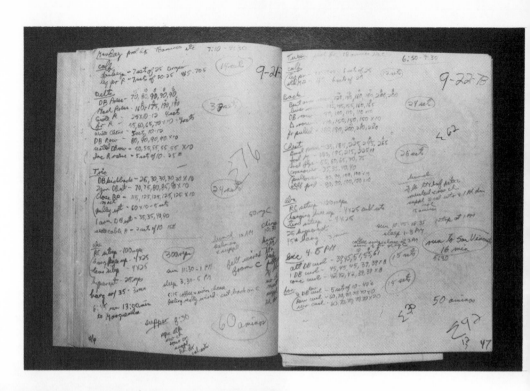

Consulting the training record.

With wife, Christine, and the trophies from the 1977 Mr. Olympia.

With Betty Weider.

BOYER COE

Boyer Coe was born at Lake Charles, Louisiana, on August 18, 1946. At the age of fifteen he proclaimed that some day he would be Mr. America. He wasn't wrong. He first won the Mr. Louisiana title in 1965, then added the titles Mr. Texas, Mr. Oklahoma, Teen-age Mr. America, Mr. America, and finally Mr. Universe.

He started weight training at age fourteen at the Lake Charles Gym, where he trained in the cold under a 100-watt light bulb. He attended college at Lafayette, Louisiana, and trained at Red Lerille's gym, where he perfected his posing. He trained there for fourteen years before opening his own gym in New Orleans.

Boyer always found time to bring his fitness philosophy to others who could not come to him. He started a training program for the state prison in Louisiana and another for the children at the Louisiana State School for the Deaf.

Boyer admits to having learned discipline and the meaning of goals from his father. This substantiates a claim that Arnold Schwarzenegger has made of champion bodybuilders—that they all had disciplined early lives. "If you think that winning a major contest will make major changes in your life, you will end up very frustrated," said Boyer's father. "You've got to do things for yourself first." Boyer has gone beyond that in his dedication to helping others.

"If you believe you will be the champion, then you have the battle half won," says Boyer. At age seventeen he bench pressed 420 in strict style. He gave up the lift because it developed too much front deltoid, causing an imbalance in his physique.

He now operates a health food store and a mail-order business, selling vitamin formulations. He travels extensively to compete and give exhibitions—he's visited Mexico, Japan, Australia, England, Germany, Austria, Trinidad, South Africa, and Singapore.

A definite superstar of the 1970s, Boyer has been a strong contender for the Mr. Olympia title. "I feel fortunate for the enjoyable experience bodybuilding has given me," he says. "Now I would like to put something back into the sport. I take every opportunity to talk before different civic groups, explaining bodybuilding and its benefits. It has come a long way since I started fifteen years ago. I hope, also, to produce many new great physiques in my gym."

To have produced Boyer Coe is testimony enough for bodybuilding.

Mr. America 1968 with runners-up, left to right: Ken Covington, Chuck Calleras, Chris Dickerson, and Gilbert Hansen.

Posing at the 1977 Mr. Olympia contest.

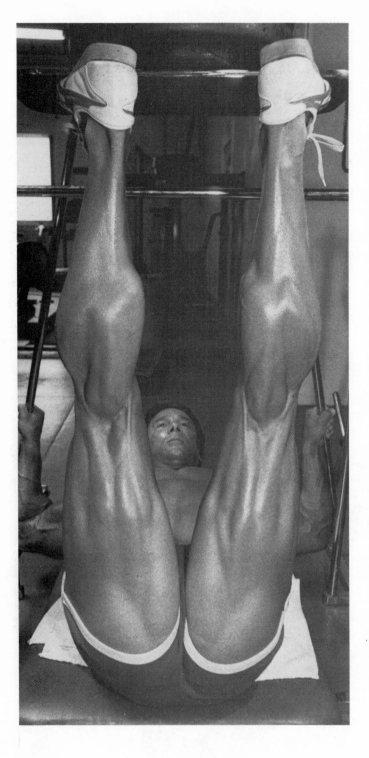

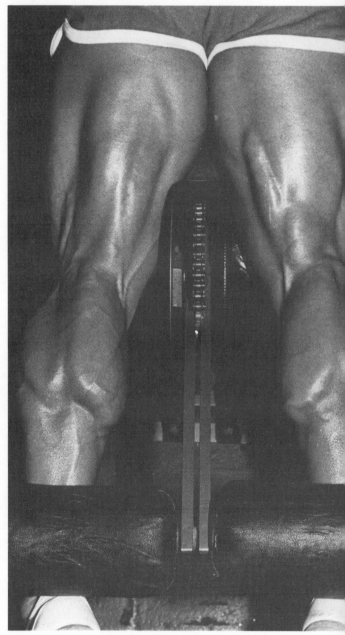

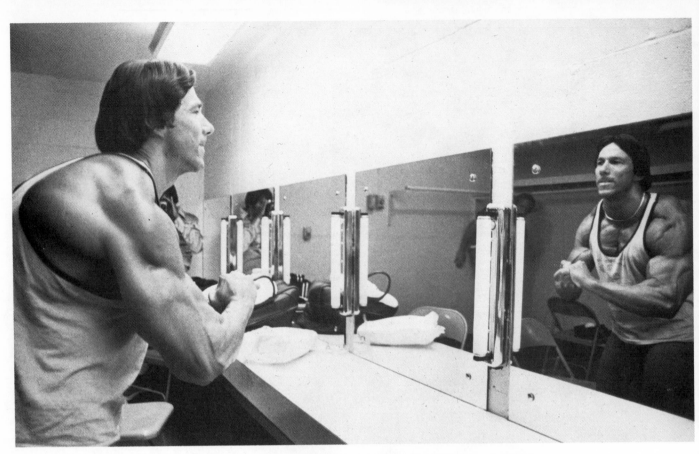

Precontest pump-up.

Wearing the Legg Shoe, of which he is codeveloper, specially designed to promote development of the calf muscles.

216

Posing at the 1978 Mr. Olympia contest.

DAN PADILLA

Dan Padilla was born of strong Puerto Rican heritage on April 1, 1951, in Rochester, New York. He went to work at age fourteen to help his parents support his ten brothers and sisters. He became a good athlete very early in life, specializing in baseball and football ("mainly to prove myself, since I was only about four-feet eleven"). At age nineteen, he carried a bowling average of 198.

Today at 5 feet 2½ inches and 175 bodyweight, Dan has been tagged "the Giant Killer," having proved conclusively that a good small man can beat a good big man, wresting national bodybuilding titles from some of the sport's most vaunted muscular mastodons.

He arrived at bodybuilding fully prepared for the challenge. He was so well built that he got away with saying he was a bodybuilder before he had ever touched a weight. Once he began training at a private barbell club in Rochester, his body quickly responded.

At age seventeen Dan won his first title, Mr. Rochester. By age twenty-two he had won all the local contests, including Mr. Atlantic Coast. He visited the West Coast, where he met Arnold Schwarzenegger, who, impressed by Dan's potential, encouraged him to go for the big titles. In 1975 Dan took the overall Mr. USA title, beating the winners of both the middle and tall classes. Two years later he won the Mr. America and Mr. Universe titles. In 1978 he placed second in the Professional World Cup contest, which Rob Robinson won.

Dan has traveled extensively at home and abroad, giving exhibitions. With bodybuilding professionalism and profit potential expanding, he is presently concentrating on bringing his physique up to the standards being set by the mightiest of the high-powered pros.

Still up and coming, still competing, Dan eventually wants to build a gym in Rochester. "I love the game, and I want to show others the right way to build their bodies," he states. "No one really helped me, and I did things wrong for many years."

He periodically returns to train in the heavily charged bodybuilding atmosphere of Santa Monica, California. Short and massive, Padilla's body is conspicuous for its perfectly shaped muscles, steep tie-ins, and peak development. It is completely suited to any pose.

219

221

Mr. USA 1975, with fellow trophy winners Roger Callard (left) and Denny Gable (right), receiving congratulations from Joe Weider.

With Boyer Coe and Ben Weider (behind Coe) en route to the 1975 Mr. Universe contest.

The disappointed competitor, denied entry in the 1975 Mr. Universe because of administrative confusion on team makeup for the United States.

USA team member for the 1976
Mr. Universe held at Montreal.

The 1977 Mr. Universe team from the United
States. Kal Szkalak (left), Danny Padilla
(center), Mike Mentzer (right).

Receiving acknowledgment as the 1977 IFBB Mr. America title winner. At left, Pete Grymkowski and Roger Callard.

Mr. America receives congratulations from Joe Weider and Franco Columbu, together with trophy winner Grymkowski. At left, Roger Callard.

Prepping for a 1978 contest.

Mr. Universe 1977.

MIKE MENTZER

Mike Mentzer comes as close to the ultimate muscleman as any bodybuilder who has ever lived. At the 1978 Mr. Universe contest in Acapulco, Mexico, he scored a perfect 300 points, becoming the first person to do so in an international championship contest. He reigns as the absolute embodiment of modern training methods and advanced nutrition concepts. At 5 feet 9 inches tall, weighing 220 pounds, he is a combination of fine structure, balanced proportions, and shapely, massive muscles. His propensity for development, by his own admission, is at least somewhat genetic—his father, without training, had 18½-inch calves.

Mike was born in Philadelphia, Pennsylvania, on November 15, 1951. He began bodybuilding at age thirteen after seeing a picture of Steve Reeves on the cover of *Muscle Builder* magazine. Though a superb young athlete, he gave up high school sports to train with weights, to the chagrin of his coaches. "I became an idolator," he said. "Bill Pearl (then Mr. Universe) became my hero."

At age nineteen Mike placed tenth at the 1971 AAU Mr. America event. A month later he placed second in the Teen-Age Mr. America, but a shoulder injury forced him out of competition for nearly three years. His bodyweight went up to 245 pounds, the result of dissipation. In 1975, after deep self-assessment, he resumed training, dropped 50 pounds in six months, and placed third in that year's IFBB Mr. America contest.

In 1976 he moved to California from Washington, D.C., where he had been studying medicine. He brought with him a totally new training concept in which he worked all body parts in ninety-minute sessions, four days a week. He had slashed the accepted weekly training time by two-thirds. Every exercise set is worked to failure, beyond normal fatigue. According to Mike, long training and hard training are mutually exclusive. The body's main concern is survival, conserving energy; it will always recover first, grow muscle second.

Mike, giving much credit for his physique to his Italian-German heritage, continues to work on infinite muscular detail. As ranking number-one amateur today, he has set his sights on lucrative pro titles such as Mr. Olympia.

He does a brisk mail-order business with his bodybuilding courses and is in great demand worldwide for exhibitions. He lives in Los Angeles.

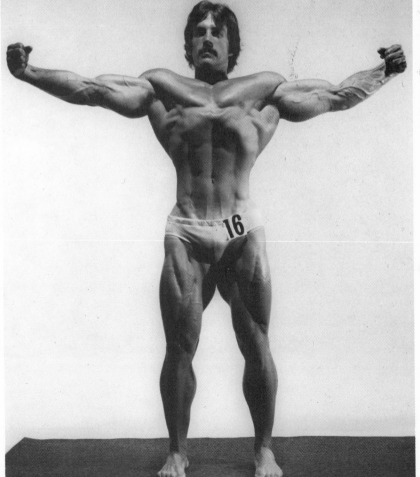

Posing at the 1977 Mr. Universe
contest in Nimes, France.

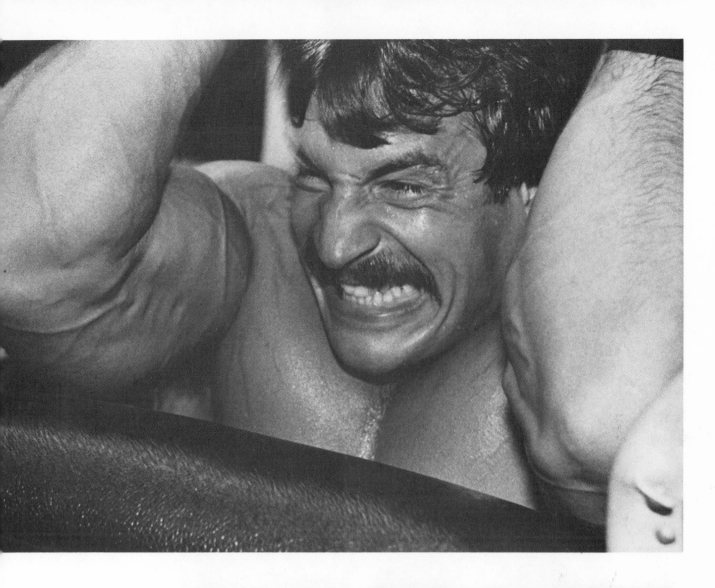

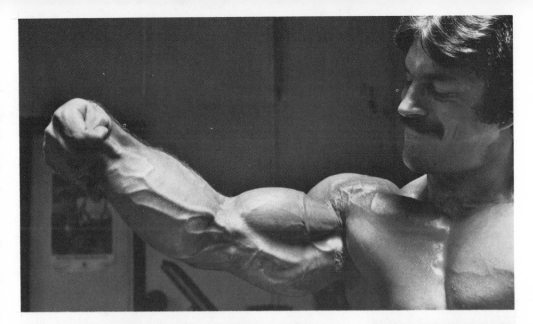

With girl friend, Cathy Gelfo (left), and women's fitness expert Mandy Tanny (right).

PHOTO CREDITS

Following is a listing of letter abbreviations appearing below: T = top, B = bottom, C = center, R = right, L = Left, TR = top right, TL = top left, BR = bottom right, BL = bottom left, CR = center right, CL = center left, CT = center top, CB = center bottom.

Studio Arax: p. 39 R
Carl R. Bakule: p. 35 TL & BL
John Balik: pp. 147 L, 149, 161 T, 209
Albert Busek: pp. 136 TR & TL, 160 B
Bruce: pp. 20, 21 TL, 40 TL, 50 L, 82 L, 83, 99 B, 100
Caruso: pp. 26 R, 27, 78, 79, 86, 87, 103, 105, 106, 107, 108, 109, 112 TL, 115, 116, 117, 123, 124 BR, 125, 134, 135, 138, 139 TL & BL, 145 R, 146, 151, 152, 153, 159 TR, 162, 163, 170 T, 171, 173 B, 188, 189 TL, 192 BL, 199, 203 C, 204, 205, 212, 213, 219, 220, 221, 222, 223, 224 T, 225, 227 BR, 229, 230 L
Constantine: pp. 15, 32 R
Benno Dahmen: pp. 127 BL, 133, 136 BL, 156, 169 T
Craig Dietz: pp. 189 BR, 234, 235, 236 L, 237, 238
H. W. Dixon: p. 101
George Valentine Enell: p. 40 R
John Evans: p. 3

George Greenwood: p. 95
International News Photo: p. 16 TR
Tony Lanza: pp. 42, 43, 44, 69, 70, 71, 72, 73, 75
Lon: pp. 19, 39 L, 49, 51 T
MGM Productions: p. 45
Gene Mozee: pp. 161 B, 181, 182
Jack Neary: pp. 189 CL & CB, 197 B
Sylvia Norris: p. 164 BL
Michael R. Neveux: p. 141
Bill Reynolds: pp. 226 T, 230 R
Schramm: pp. 53 BR, 101
Lennie Sirmopolous: p. 216 B
Spartan of Hollywood: pp. 16 BL, 33, 46 T, 50 R, 51 B
Hal Stephens: p. 53 BL
Leo Stern: p. 98
Swan Photo: p. 210
Russ Warner: pp. 24, 26 L, 29, 34, 41, 58, 59, 60, 61, 64, 65, 66 TR, 76, 77, 92, 93, 94, 160 T, 192 CR, 226 B, 231
Warner Brothers: p. 47
Trevor A. Webster: p. 32 L, 113 B
Douglas White: p. 21 B, 120 TL, 139 CR, 143 R
Art Zeller: pp. 85, 126, 127 TR, 130, 137, 144 T, 145 TL & BL, 157, 158, 159 BL, 164 BR, 167, 168 BR, 169 B, 170 B, 172, 173 T, 174 T, 175 B, 176, 178, 179 CR, 186, 187, 193 TR & BL, 194 TL

The credits for the color insert are as follows in the order of appearance: Russ Warner, Caruso, Art Zeller, Bob Gardner, Caruso, Bob Gardner, Universal Studios, Art Zeller, John Balik, John Balik, Bill Reynolds, Russ Warner, Craig Dietz, Bob Gardner, Bob Gardner, John Balik.